Tolkien in Translation

edited by
Thomas Honegger

2011

Cormarë Series No. 4

Series Editors: Peter Buchs • Thomas Honegger • Andrew Moglestue • Johanna Schön

Library of Congress Cataloging-in-Publication Data

Honegger, Thomas
Tolkien in Translation
ISBN 978-3-905703-15-3

Subject headings:
Tolkien, J.R.R. (John Ronald Reuel), 1892-1973 - Criticism and interpretation
Tolkien, J.R.R. (John Ronald Reuel), 1892-1973 - Language
Translation
Literature, Comparative

First published 2003
Second edition 2011

Cormarë Series No. 4

© Walking Tree Publishers, Zurich and Jena, 2003, 2011

All rights reserved. No portion of this book may be reproduced, by any process or technique, without the express written consent of the publisher

Cover illustration: "Journey to Rivendell", Anke Eißmann 2005

Set in Adobe Garamond Pro and Shannon by Walking Tree Publishers
Printed by Lightning Source in the United Kingdom and United States

Editor's Preface

Public interest in the work of J.R.R. Tolkien has reached new peaks in the second year after the release of the first part of Peter Jackson's adaptation of *The Lord of the Rings*. This is felt, in my case, also on a professional level – I have never before been invited for so many guest lectures on Tolkien. Public demand for elucidation and expounding on all levels has been great indeed.

Furthermore, the piecemeal presentation of the tale has motivated many a moviegoer to turn to the book in order to alleviate the suspense of a cliffhanger plot. Since the language of Tolkien's epic is, admittedly, not very easy even for those readers whose command of English is above average, translations have become of vital importance. Yet it is a well-known truth that a translation is, at best, only an approximation of the original.

The contributions united in this volume are original studies that deal with a wide range of problems and challenges connected with the task of translating Tolkien's work. They offer not only in-depth discussions of translations into various languages (sometimes based on first-hand experience), but also provide more general theoretical examinations of translation strategies. The brief abstracts that precede each article will help the reader to find the paper of his or her choice.

Thomas Honegger

Jena, Spring 2003

Acknowledgments

I would like to express my thanks to all the contributors for their co-operation and patience during all stages of the preparation of the manuscript.

I would also like to thank Jana Pfeiffer and Kathrin Prietzel who proofread the articles with great care.

Finally, I wish to express my gratitude to Walking Tree Publishers for making this venture possible.

Tolkien in Translation

Contents

Editor's Preface	i
Acknowledgments	ii
A Theoretical Model for Tolkien Translation Criticism *Allan Turner*	1
A Question of Style On Translating *The Silmarillion* into Norwegian *Nils Ivar Agøy*	31
Traduire Tolkien en Français: On the Translation of J.R.R. Tolkien's Works into French and their Reception in France *Vincent Ferré, Daniel Lauzon, David Riggs*	45
Begging your pardon, Con el perdón de usted: Some Socio-Linguistic Features in *The Lord of the Rings* in English and Spanish *Sandra Bayona*	69
The Treatment of Names in Esperanto Translations of Tolkien's Works *Arden R. Smith*	91
Nine Russian Translations of *The Lord of the Rings* *Mark T. Hooker*	119

Allan Turner

A Theoretical Model for Tolkien Translation Criticism

Abstract

This article outlines a possible theoretical model to serve as a basis for criticism of translations of Tolkien's Middle-earth cycle, adapted from the 'hermeneutic motion' of George Steiner and considering both text-internal and socio-economic constraints on the translator. It argues that Tolkien's published comments on translation cannot be accepted uncritically as authoritative, but need to be justified in the light of the overall literary and linguistic structure of the books, particularly the text-world and the pseudotranslation device.

1 Introduction

At a time when Tolkien's fame and popularity worldwide is on the increase, partly as a result of the well-publicised film version of *The Lord of the Rings* by Peter Jackson, we are likely to see his works translated into yet more languages, while some existing translations may be replaced by new ones. In this situation, Tolkien enthusiasts are likely to want to make a critical comparison of different versions, either between the version in their language and the source text, or between old and new versions in the same target language.

Readers who are very familiar with a particular text will already have a good idea of what they like and what they do not, and will formulate their criticisms accordingly. However, while *ad hoc* opinions, supported by reasoning on the lines of "That's not what Tolkien meant", or even "But Tolkien says so in his notes for translators", may be clear to other Tolkien enthusiasts, they may need some justification if they are to be accepted by a wider readership. Such justification can be provided by a model which identifies criteria that are particularly relevant to the literary and linguistic structures of Tolkien's writings, but which can also be viewed within a more general theory of translation to counter claims that he is being treated as a special case. To avoid unfair *ad hominem* criticism, the theory should also allow for consideration of the practice of translation and the social and professional setting in which it is carried out.

One advantage of a theoretical model is that it can help to distinguish between cases that are governed by a general principle and those which are purely incidental. For example, some translations contain a high proportion of misprints, so that on several occasions Éomer appears in the French version as *Eomir*, while occasionally a sentence or a part of a sentence is missed out. These are mistakes caused by lapses of concentration, and are more likely to be the fault of the typesetter than of the translator; after all, it took many years to establish an English text of *The Lord of the Rings* free of printing errors. Then there are cases where an unusual idiom, which would be obvious to a native speaker used to the author's diction, is simply misunderstood, which can happen occasionally even in translation of the highest quality. If the object of the criticism is to provide a basis for a revision of the text, then it is perfectly legitimate to point out incidental errors of this kind. But criticism based on clear principles will do more: it will allow us to say something meaningful about Tolkien's artistic design.

This article proposes such a model, which may help to formalise criticism of Tolkien translations. It was devised specifically for *The Lord of the Rings*, since this offers the most complex linguistic and literary patterning, and also the most explicit statements about language, but it can be applied equally to *The Hobbit*, *The Silmarillion*, and even to some extent to *The Adventures of Tom Bombadil*, since by associating all of these with the 'Red Book of Westmarch' Tolkien brought them under the umbrella of the pseudotranslation device which will be explained in detail below. It will call upon the resources of linguistics, literary criticism and translation studies, although it will try not to assume too much specialist knowledge of these fields. There is a well-established history of high quality do-it-yourself criticism amongst Tolkien readers, largely as a result of the lack of interest shown by many professional critics, which has been extended into the field of translation by the well-publicised campaign of the Deutsche Tolkien-Gesellschaft to stimulate a critical debate about the new German translation of *The Lord of the Rings*. It is hoped that this article may be of use in continuing the tradition.

2 The General Theory

The basic model adopted here will be that of Steiner (1998), who characterises it as the 'hermeneutic motion'. He identifies four stages in "the elicitation and appropriative transfer of meaning" (p. 312) as trust, aggression, incorporation, and compensation. Stripped of some of Steiner's layers of metaphor, this can be interpreted roughly as follows:

A. Before the translation can even begin, there must be a belief that there is something which is of value for the target culture, otherwise it would be pointless to translate it in the first place.
B. Next, the translator must penetrate to the depths of the source text in order to appropriate the whole meaning, which is the in-depth reading stage.
C. This meaning must then be brought home, that is to say, assimilated to the linguistic and ideological structures of the target language.
D. Finally, balance must be restored as the foreign object is assimilated, that is to say the target text ceases to stand out as something exotic but becomes a part of the target culture.

It must be stressed that this is not an empirical description of the act of translation, nor is it a pedagogical method. However, it is a metaphor which emphasizes in a very powerful way the need for translators to engage at depth with the whole complexity of the design of the work, in this case Tolkien's highly detailed structure of *The Lord of the Rings*. Since Steiner is considering not so much the methodology of the individual translator as the communal, even unconscious motions of the whole linguistic and cultural group, Stage C, which corresponds to the traditional, informal concept of translation, is only one part of the whole process. Stage B, concerning the translator's own understanding gained from a detailed reading and interpretation of the source text[1], will be related in detail to aspects of literary analysis and the status of the author to form the longest section, section 4. Stages B and C of Steiner's model are the ones which will concern us most here, since they embody the task of the translator and call upon his or her particular skill. However, Stages A and D set the background to the wider social field within which the whole translation process takes place, so it will be convenient to explain them together first.

---

1 The work to be translated is usually known in translation studies as the source text, while any translation is a target text, since this shows the direction of the process. We can also talk of source and target languages.

3 Stages A and D – Social Constraints

The principle of 'trust' underlying Stage A is fundamental to most theories of communication: before I can seek to understand what you are trying to signify to me, I have first to believe that the sounds you are uttering, or the gestures you are making, or the marks made by you on the paper are in some way meaningful and relevant to my situation. In the context of a work of literature that is to be translated for publication, the assessment of the value of the source text is likely to be as much the task of the publisher as of the translator. Issues involved include the perceived status of the author and work in as far as they are known in the target culture, also the genre, and how the new work will fit into the publisher's existing list. Other decisions may concern the inclusion of illustrations or appendices. Such considerations may influence the work of the translator – for example, if a book is specifically commissioned for a children's series, it may be given to a specialist children's translator, who will apply particular pedagogical criteria, while if it is already an acknowledged classic it may be treated with more care than if it is unknown – but will not necessarily be under his or her direct control.

Stage D, which apparently closes the cycle, is concerned with the reception of the target text in the target culture, and is both an end and a beginning. If the translation is successful enough to sell in large numbers, it is likely that the work will become so well known, possibly in the original language too, that the general critical understanding of it becomes modified and the old translation is perceived to be inadequate. If it remains popular for long enough, then the idiom of the translation may come to be seen as outdated. In such cases a new translation may be called for. But by now, paradoxically, the first translation may be so established in the target culture that it is perceived as normative, and the new translation meets with resistance regardless of its merits or demerits. This has been seen in the case of the new German translation of *The Lord of the Rings* by Krege, in which the translator has to admit in an afterword (Tolkien 2000:379f.) that he has taken over the wording of his predecessor in places where in his opinion it could not be improved on. In particular he has kept the proper names in most cases, which reflects their special quality as words of unique reference, but also perhaps the way in which the plethora of such details has led to their acceptance as unalterable givens or 'facts' among Tolkien's readers, so that even the apparently minor change of *Butterblume* 'Butterbur' to *Butterblüm* has provoked controversy in some quarters.

It is important to remember that translation takes place at a particular point in time and proposes only a provisional solution; there is no such thing as a perfect and definitive translation. The translator's task is to present the text in a way that is both accessible and acceptable to the target readership at the time and place where it is published. If the public rejects the translation, then the translator has failed both them and the author. That is why translation theorists highlight the role of the translator as one of mediation; Jones (2000) uses the metaphor of an ambassador, whose task it is to represent his government and its policies in the best possible light to the host country. This may even involve doing what a later generation perceives as falsifying what the author has to say. For example, Lefevere (1998) demonstrates how, in order to make Brecht acceptable to American audiences, the earlier translators modified the forms of his epic theatre and cut out any references to Marxist ideology. The justification for this is that at least it allowed something of Brecht's plays to become known in the target culture, preparing the way for a more faithful translation when the political and cultural climate had changed, leading to a new critical appreciation of the author. The same principle may perhaps be seen at work in the Swedish translation of *The Lord of the Rings* by Ohlmarks. Faced by what must have seemed a strange genre with mysterious references to a complex background mythology, he attempted to interpret these references to make them more comprehensible for his readers. Unfortunately he did that at a time when *The Silmarillion* was not available to guide his guesses, and before Tolkien criticism, working from ideas in the published letters, had appreciated Tolkien's literary technique of the broad and only partially explained historical vista (see below). For example, in Strider's story of Beren and Lúthien at Weathertop, he translates "they met again beyond the Sundering Seas" as "de möttes igen bortom 'det vida hav', dödens ocean som skiljer liv från liv" (they met again beyond 'the wide sea', the ocean of death that separates life from life – AT). Whether it was appropriate for the translator to make such interpretations in 1959 is a matter for critical debate. Whether it is appropriate for the Swedish publisher to offer this as the only available version over 40 years later is a completely different question.

One area where the reception of the book has brought about changes is the provision of the Appendices. When *The Lord of the Rings* was first published, they must have seemed something totally foreign to the accepted genre of the novel. Even Tolkien himself had some reservations at the time, as he said in reply to his publisher, who was also concerned about their sheer length and tried to insist on cuts:

> I now wish that no appendices had been promised! For I think their appearance in truncated and compressed form will satisfy nobody: certainly not me; clearly from the (appalling mass of) letters I receive not those people who like that kind of thing – astonishingly many; while those who enjoy the book as an 'heroic romance' only, and find 'unexplained vistas' part of the literary effect, will neglect the appendices, very properly. (Tolkien 1981:210)

Different translations have varied as to whether they include all the Appendices, or just a selection, or none at all, although the Prologue has been included in most, perhaps because it contains useful preliminary information and forms a link with *The Hobbit*. It may also be that background information is more acceptable at the beginning than at the end, after the dénouement has been reached and a conventional novel or play might be considered finished. But the decision about what to include probably lies in the hands of the publishers as much as the translators, and may hang on non-literary considerations. Certainly the Swedish publishers were dubious about their inclusion, and Tolkien's opinion was sought by Allen and Unwin. He suggested that they were desirable for the literary effect, but was prepared to agree that the extra cost involved might be prohibitive (Tolkien 1981:304).

In fact a number of translations were first published with none of the Appendices apart from an extract from Appendix A, 'A Part of the Tale of Aragorn and Arwen'. This is the form of the first British one-volume paperback, published in 1968 and available for over 20 years (Hammond and Anderson 1993:142f.), which appeared in Tolkien's lifetime and was presumably sanctioned by him. It illustrates how one particular version which is not necessarily the 'standard' edition in the source language may become the accepted form of the target text. However, the demands of readers familiar with the full source text, or at least with its list of contents, have often led to the translation of some or all of the Appendices at a later date. This is the case with the French editions, where the 1972 translation by Francis Ledoux was supplemented in 1986 by the complete Appendices translated by Tina Jolas (Hammond and Anderson 1993:393), where unfortunately the change of translator led to a number of discrepancies. So also it has come about that beside the standard three-volume paperback German, Dutch and Swedish editions (as opposed to some bound single-volume editions) there appeared a separate volume devoted to the Appendices. It is notable that the new German (2000) translation keeps this arrangement, with the Appendices offered in an identical format but not as a part of the three-volume boxed set, so it may be considered to have become 'canonised', at least in Germany.

The nature of the Appendices is central for how the translator understands Tolkien's complex network of linguistic relationships, and will be discussed in detail in sections 4.3 to 4.5. Here, the question of their inclusion serves as a reminder of the main points regarding the external constraints that apply to translation:

1. Book publishing is guided by economic considerations as much as by aesthetic ones.
2. In the case of an unfamiliar work, considerations of what is appropriate or acceptable for a particular genre in the target culture may lead to modifications of the text.
3. Changes in critical opinion, which may be led either by professional critics or by the general public, may call for a new translation, or an extensive revision of the old one.

If ever in the discussion of Stages B and C of Steiner's model it appears that criteria are being set up for an ideal translation, it will be useful to refer back to these constraints, which extend over all considerations of detail.

4 Stage B – Understanding the Literary Text

This section considers aspects of the translator's detailed reading of the source text, and in particular what status and authority can be accorded to Tolkien's own stated intentions. It is assumed that any professional literary translator has a thorough knowledge of the structure and idiom of the source language, as well as being familiar with a wide range of literary styles, but Tolkien's command of a range of historical styles and interplay of philological correspondences often poses special problems. But in addition to applying linguistic knowledge, the translator is also seeking to gain a detailed understanding of how the source text functions as a work of literature. Although there are some important differences, as will be seen, this part of the task is very similar to that of the literary critic, and can call upon some of the same professional tools.

In the case of Tolkien translation criticism, potential critics will no doubt also be familiar with the secondary literature, particularly the two books by Shippey (1992 and 2000), which relate the literary structure closely to the author's interest in language. However, they will probably want to make reference first and foremost to Tolkien's own writings about translation, particularly Appendix F of *The Lord of the Rings*, the 'Guide to Names' (Tolkien 1975), and the relevant published letters. But these cannot be used uncritically, without considering to what extent they may be regarded as authoritative. Therefore the first part of this section examines the question of authorial intention, and attempts to outline a relationship between literary criticism and translation theory. The second part introduces the two concepts of 'text-world' and 'pseudotranslation', which link issues in translation with the particular literary structure of the work in question.

4.1 The status of the author

It is reasonable to assume that, all other things being equal in the target culture, a translator will wish to transmit as much as possible of the literary design of the source text into the target language. Nevertheless it may be useful at this point to consider briefly the more general question of how far the stated intention of an author should be considered binding upon translators, or more relevantly, whether it is appropriate to value a translation which follows his stated wishes more highly than one which does not. This question is bound up with debates amongst both literary critics and translation theorists about the status of the author.

During the Romantic period and through its aftermath the question would have seemed pointless; the cult of the artist placed the creative writer, together with the composer, the painter and the sculptor, on a pedestal and looked up to him for guidance. But in the course of the 20th century this pre-eminent position was brought more and more into doubt. In the English-speaking world the poet T.S. Eliot relativised the influence of the individual talent against that of tradition, while the influential critics Richards and Leavis, with the express intention of leaving behind what seemed to many to be an excessively subjective and unsystematic approach to literature, insisted on the central importance of a close reading of the text. According to this outlook, only the words as they appear on the page can form the basis for criticism. It is senseless to judge a work of literature on what its writer's intention might be thought to be (the 'intentional fallacy'), since the workings of other people's minds are not open to scrutiny, while if a writer attempts to explain his work, he is simply performing an act of literary criticism like any other critic and cannot claim any privileged status.

Amongst the different schools of literary criticism, it is worth briefly mentioning the hermeneutic approach here because of its relevance to Steiner's 'hermeneutic motion' which provides the model for this discussion. For hermeneuticist critics the situation is not so simple, since meaning is both objective and subjective. Hirsch makes a distinction between the 'meaning' of a work, which is identical to what the author meant by it at the time of writing, and 'significance', which is the way in which any individual interprets it at any given time. The corollary of this is that "[t]here may be a number of valid interpretations, but all of them must move within the 'system of typical expectations and probabilities' which the author's meaning permits" (Eagleton 1983:67).

This view seems to be entirely compatible with Tolkien's own statement in the Foreword to the second edition of *The Lord of the Rings*, in which he rebuts those critics who have attempted to see in the story an allegory of the Second World War or any other recent period of history:

> But I cordially dislike allegory in all its manifestations, and always have done so since I grew old and wary enough to detect its presence. I much prefer history, true or feigned, with its varied applicability to the thought and experience of readers. I think that many confuse 'applicability' with 'allegory'; but the one resides in the freedom of the reader, and the other in the purposed domination of the author. (Tolkien 1992:11)

It is true that symbolic meaning is only a part of the whole network of meanings that are possible within a text, but nevertheless Tolkien here draws attention to the limited possibilities for individual understanding within the overall limits of what the author can be considered to mean.

However, the critical standpoints adopted both by the close-reading school and by Hirsch ultimately depend upon an acceptance that a text enshrines a particular meaning created by its author. This tenet came under attack in the last third of the 20th century from approaches derived from the structuralist linguistics of Saussure, but finding their clearest and most uncompromising statement in the post-structuralism of the decade after 1968, the icon for which is Roland Barthes' essay, 'The Death of the Author'. In brief, these are founded on the premise that it is impossible for the addressee to derive the full range of significance in the mind of the addresser from the linguistic sign (i.e. the spoken or written word), so all meaning, including that of literary texts, is something constructed by the addressee (or reader) from the information available, and is essentially pluralistic; there is no given meaning. This, from a critical point of view at least, would remove the author from any position of authority.

But what is useful for literary criticism may be much less so for translation theory. If the critical voices are contradictory as regards the status of the author, then what else could guide the translator in deciding how far to follow the author's voice? After all, the translator has to face a different set of decisions: the critic may opt for multiple interpretations, but the translator normally has to produce just one target text which will enshrine the interpretative decision he or she has made in each particular instance. In fact in the case of contemporary literature it is quite usual for a translator to work closely with an author, particularly in translating poetry, although of course there can be points of disagreement, and the translator has the balancing authority of a greater knowledge of the target language, as well as the culture which may provide its own constraints, as demonstrated in section 3 above. This seems to suggest that in translation there may be a valid part for both the author and the translator to play. They may even complement one another, in that the author may clarify ideas for the translator, and within the context of literary ambiguity and pluralistic readings the translator may be helping to create the meaning(s) of the text in the target culture. However, instead of merely accepting Tolkien's prescriptions as given, we should attempt to justify them by deciding whether they are arbitrary or whether they are derived from the exigencies of the linguistic and literary structure of the book. The argument will be based on the two concepts of 'text-world' and 'pseudotranslation'.

4.2 The text-world

It is a basic assumption amongst most linguists that all texts, with the possible exception of some short sentences invented purely to exemplify a linguistic point, presuppose a context. Some linguists differentiate between 'co-text', meaning the linguistic information given in the immediate vicinity of the textual point in question, and 'context', referring to the receptor's broader assumptions about the world. Different types of source text will require the translator to have access to different types of information in order to ensure that the translation fits into the necessary context; for example, in technical translation it might be necessary to refer to specialist dictionaries and manuals, or even to seek specific advice from an expert in that field. However, in dealing with a work of fiction we may be faced with places and situations which are completely invented and outside not only our personal experience but also the resources of reference books. In some genres such as fantasy and science fiction it is not unusual even to find invented words, or already existing words used in a special sense so that they have no referent in the 'real' world. Invented worlds may well display patterns of thought different from those to be found in known cultures. In dealing with contexts in such fictional works it may be convenient to use the term 'text-world' to mean the set of contexts available within that text, or within a group of related texts. It corresponds closely to Tolkien's own term 'Secondary World', but the more general term will be preferred here, because it could be applied just as well to a fictional work in the realist tradition, such as Trollope's Barsetshire novels, which are centred upon social relationships in a fictitious English county. Usually there will be sufficient information about the text-world in the text itself to make it comprehensible for the reader, although of course much more can be left to inference if it is set in a recognisable historical period. However, in any case the only 'specialist' who possesses all the information is the author.

This applies particularly in Tolkien's case, since he worked out over a period of about half a century a highly detailed text-world which came to form the background not just to *The Lord of the Rings* but also to *The Hobbit* and *The Silmarillion*. Although the Elvish histories of *The Silmarillion* were not published until after Tolkien's death, he had been working on them for over twenty years when *The Lord of the Rings* was begun, and they provide a constant backdrop of myth and legend against which the action of the tale is set, but a backdrop which is often highly allusive. The Appendices help to fill in some of the background of this text-world, but by no means all, and indeed sometimes introduce problems of their own. This structure provides pitfalls into which the translator might unwittingly fall, particularly in the days before the publication of *The Silmarillion*, since many innocent-seeming words may contain a text-world philological reference to the ancient past which will need to be interpreted.

Some examples may make clear the scope for different degrees of error when dealing with a text-world that is incompletely known to the translator, or even not completely knowable. In any kind of translation, it is clear that some things can be unequivocally labelled as mistakes. In a whole range of text-types, it is possible to misunderstand a word, expression or broader context in the source text and introduce an error of fact while still producing a coherent translation, the situational incongruity of which may not be noticed, or may even be taken as part of the original intention. There are other errors of translation which might have been corrected by reference to a dictionary or grammar, or by comparison with another point in the text. In the real world of technical translation, such mistakes may prove expensive both to the client and to the translator, or at least to their insurers. Descriptive translation studies may regard them as trivial, but they are nevertheless errors of fact which should be corrected in any subsequent revision.

To apply this principle to *The Lord of the Rings*, it cannot be any other than a hasty misreading when the French translator renders "Not West but East does our doom await us" as "C'est à l'Ouest et non à l'Est que notre destin nous attend" (II, 166) (It is to the West and not to the East that our doom awaits us – AT), although even the few readers who noticed its incongruity at that point in the narrative could somehow interpret the context to make the utterance relevant. When he misinterprets "Isildur Elendil's son" as "[le] fils d'Isildur Elendil", apparently deceived by Tolkien's stylistic omission of a comma into mistaking *Elendil* for a surname, he could have corrected himself in the course of subsequent revision by noting from the many other references that Isildur and Elendil are separate characters and Elendil is Isildur's father. This is an error of fact within the text-world.

But what about when, under a similar misapprehension, he translates "Dior Thingol's heir" as "l'héritier de Dior Thingol" (and is followed by the Spanish translator with "el heredero de Dior Thingol")? It might be argued that there is enough implicit information in the immediate co-text to suggest that this interpretation is highly unlikely, but an unambiguous reference to Dior's parentage is given only in Appendix A, which is not included in either translation, and indeed might not even have been read by the translators. The full story is told only in *The Silmarillion*.

To take a more complex example, the Swedish translator, working before the publication of *The Silmarillion*, and with a tendency to interpret as we have seen, translates the origin of the White Tree "out of the Uttermost West in the Day before days when the world was young" as "från det Yttersta Västerness en gång i tidernas början" (from Uttermost Westernesse once in the beginning of time – AT). In fact there are two points here. The more easily demonstrable error in text-world terms is that in the mythology the Uttermost West, the abode of the Valar, is completely different both in geography and in significance from Westernesse (Númenor), an island inhabited by mortals, as can be ascertained (possibly with the benefit of hindsight) by a careful reading of the text of *The Lord of the Rings*, particularly the Appendices. Furthermore, it may be concluded from a careful study of *The Silmarillion* and the volumes of *The History of Middle-earth* that the "Day before days" has a specific meaning in Tolkien's mythology, so the translator has produced a levelling effect by paraphrasing it. But the essential point remains that only the author can give authoritative information, and if it is to be found outside the text that is being translated, then that gives a special status to his other writings, whether literary or non-literary.

4.3 The pseudotranslation structure

Relatively little attention has been paid in the critical literature to the presentation of *The Lord of the Rings* as a pseudotranslation, that is to say it is offered to the reader as if it were an edition of an ancient manuscript that has been 'translated' from the original language or languages by the 'editor'. In his entry 'Pseudotranslation' in the *Routledge Encyclopedia of Translation Studies* (Baker 1998:183ff.), Douglas Robinson differentiates (here slightly simplified) between the intentional fraud of original work which is passed off as a translation in order to deceive the public, as exemplified by Macpherson's *Ossian*, and a literary device related to the "'found-manuscript' conceit" used by novelists to give their work an aura of authenticity. As an example of the latter he cites Cervantes, who claims that *Don Quixote* is a translation from an Arabic writer called El Cid Benegali. According to Robinson, in doing this he is "playfully putting distance between himself and his own literary creation in order simultaneously to enhance and to undermine its authenticity as a record of fact".

Clearly *The Lord of the Rings* belongs in the latter category, since its author has no intention of deceiving the public, and just like Cervantes he is using verisimilitude, the carefully created illusion of truth, to achieve a particular artistic effect. Therefore it is necessary to explain from a literary-critical point of view how and why the device is used in order to demonstrate how it may provide problems for the translator. Shippey (1992:105f.) devotes two paragraphs to the chain of reasoning which probably led Tolkien to adopt it, but as yet there has been no thorough study of the literary and linguistic relationship between the text, that is to say the tale itself, and what will be referred to here as the metatext (i.e. text about the text), so for lack of anything more detailed to refer to, the explanation here is necessarily rather lengthy. To the Tolkien expert a large amount of this may seem self-evident, but nevertheless a formal statement of it is necessary if it is to form the basis of translation criticism.

In fact the machinery of the pseudotranslation in *The Lord of the Rings* is particularly complex and takes in the other works by Tolkien which share the same text-world. The story is presented as a translation of a manuscript purported to be a copy of the original memoirs of Bilbo and Frodo. The format is made to resemble that of an academic edition of a real-world ancient text, not unlike Tolkien and Gordon's edition of the Middle English poem *Sir Gawain and the Green Knight*, where the poem is presented together with a scholarly apparatus consisting of an introduction to the manuscript tradition, notes on individual words and phrases, and a glossary. The pseudo-scholarly introduction by an 'editor'-persona, reflecting Tolkien's professional activity as a philologist, was a favourite device of his, being used with considerable wit and whimsy in *Farmer Giles of Ham*, and later in *The Adventures of Tom Bombadil*, where its function is to tie in some of his earlier and unrelated poems with the text-world of Middle-earth. It is certainly not an original invention of his; a rudimentary form of it is to be found as an introduction to Scott's *Ivanhoe*, the first popular English historical romance. But in *The Lord of the Rings* the proportion of metatext is far greater than in most other works using the same device, with 1036 pages of narrative set against 118 pages of Prologue and Appendices, or a ratio of about 10:1.

The metatext consists of a Prologue and six Appendices, the last of which, and the most important here, namely Appendix F, is subdivided into two sections. There are also a number of footnotes to the main text which may be regarded as metatextual. For purely practical purposes, the Prologue is there to act as a link between *The Hobbit* and *The Lord of the Rings*, giving necessary background information for readers who have not read the earlier book, but at the same time subtly shifting and extending the text-world for those who have. The Appendices provide a large amount of additional historical, geographical, linguistic and cultural information about the text-world, including some references to the events of the then unpublished *Silmarillion*. But what is of importance for translators in their detailed reading of the text is on the one hand the literary function of this vast edifice, and on the other the very particular contents of Appendix F II, 'On Translation'.

4.4 The literary function of the metatext

The huge metatext has been regarded by some as a kind of non-literary monstrosity; Brooke-Rose, after criticising "the 'hypertrophic' redundancy in the text itself", dismisses the Appendices as "[not] in the least necessary to the narrative, but they have given much infantile happiness to the Tolkien clubs and societies"

(1981:247; quoted in Shippey 1992:283). Shippey refutes this argument, having shown all through his book that the wealth of detail is responsible for the impression of reality and historical depth which is characteristic of *The Lord of the Rings*. But other critics, including those well disposed to Tolkien, have simply ignored the Appendices as extraneous to the 'real' work. For the sake of the translator's reading, they need to be placed clearly in their literary context.

The metatext can definitely be seen to form an integral part of the literary work, for two clear reasons, based on the ideas of text-world and pseudotranslation as set out above. The first is that they are devoted to the subject matter of the text-world, which is viewed entirely from within the pseudotranslation frame. The second is that the narrative voice of the Appendices is unambiguously that of a literary persona; not the same as the narrator of the main text, but an 'editor' (who is also a 'translator' because of the pseudotranslation device) who claims to have compiled the tale from an old manuscript. That is to say, the main tale is a feigned history, while the Prologue and Appendices represent a feigned work of philology which is no less a part of the fiction. The 'editor' consistently treats the material as reality, so he can be regarded as being in a 'wider text-world'. Only in the Foreword does the author speak with his own voice, stepping outside the 'editor' persona and treating *The Lord of the Rings* as a work of his own creation; for this reason it will not be considered a part of the metatext.

This distinction between the text-world and the real world is an important one for Tolkien, based on his particular conception of fantasy and how it gains its effect. It is significant that the Foreword as we have it dates from the second edition of 1966. The original Foreword did in fact mingle the text-world viewpoint with that of the real world, using the voices of both the author and the 'editor'. Tolkien noted in one of his copies:

> This Foreword I should wish very much in any case to cancel. Confusing (as it does) real personal matters with the "machinery" of the Tale is a serious mistake. (Tolkien 1996:26)

The same punctiliousness extended to the writing of blurbs, which Tolkien clearly regarded as belonging closely to the text and not just as extraneous advertising copy. Concerning the one devised for a British paperback edition of *The Hobbit*, he wrote to his publisher:

> Unless you wish to defeat the 'magic', you should NEVER talk like this within the covers of a marvellous tale. *The Hobbit* saga is presented as *vera historia*, at great pains (which have proved very effective). In that frame the question 'Are you a hobbit?' can only be answered 'No' or 'Yes', according to one's birth. (Tolkien 1981:365)

This stricture is based on the principle which underlies the whole of Tolkien's fantasy writing, an awareness of which is important for the translator. It is stated in the essay *On Fairy-stories*, as a counter-argument to Coleridge's idea of the "willing suspension of disbelief". Tolkien removes the onus of the illusion from the reader to the writer, who creates a Secondary World into which the mind of the reader can enter:

> Inside it, what he relates is 'true': it accords with the laws of that world. You therefore believe it, while you are, as it were, inside. The moment disbelief arises, the spell is broken; the magic, or rather art, has failed. (Tolkien 1964:36)

It is this insistence on absolute consistency in adhering to the laws of the Secondary World, in our case the text-world of *The Lord of the Rings*, that lies at the heart of Tolkien's mastery of the fantasy genre which he himself did so much to create. The pseudotranslation device is not essential to it, since the tale would be true to its own internal laws even without that, but the metatext underlines the special workings of the Secondary World by demonstrating them more fully. An awareness of the principle may help to guide translators when making choices in their target text; anyone who wishes to contravene it should be very aware of what they are doing and of the effect on the overall literary design that this may cause.

4.5 The linguistic structure

As might be expected in a pseudotranslation, the two chief difficulties posed to a translator by the metatext are of a metalinguistic nature and are encountered in Appendices E, 'Writing and Spelling', F I, 'The Languages and Peoples of the Third Age', and F II, 'On Translation'. The first concerns the translation of those sections alone, while the second, far more fundamental one involves linguistic relationships throughout the whole book.

The problem in translation is that all the discussion of text-world linguistics relates it specifically to English as the language of the original, source text reader, as well as that of the philologist 'editor'. Therefore the translator has to decide between translating literally and leaving the reader to work out the correspondences between the relevant features of the target language and English (not as the source language but as a *tertium comparationis*, which would severely complicate the reading for non-linguists), and turning the target language into the basis of the linguistic comments, which may necessitate some radical changes to the source text. This problem is obviously most marked in Appendix F II, the section dealing specifically with translation (sc. from the putative text-world languages into English).

Appendix F II is in fact a complex literary and linguistic *tour de force* which operates on several levels. While remaining essentially in the wider text-world like all the Appendices, that is to say treating the world of the story as historical fact, at the same time it creates for the reader the illusion of a direct link through time and space with his/her own world through the persona of the 'editor' as he explains the procedure of using different registers of modern literary English for the characterisation of different individuals and races, as well as introducing the related Old English and Old Norse to represent related languages in the text-world. This illusion is partly the result of analogy, including a reference to the real-world philology of Middle English literature, but one which uses the figure of Arthur, who stands somewhere between history and legend, blurring the distinction between reality and fiction even more:

> But to refer to Rivendell as Imladris was as if one now was to speak of Winchester as Camelot, except that the identity was certain, while in Rivendell there still dwelt a lord of renown far older than Arthur would be, were he still king at Winchester today. (Tolkien 1992:1168)

In fact this Appendix is omitted in almost all the translations because of the complexities that it presents. A theoretical justification of this practice can be found in section 6.

But in the end this is really no more than a linguistic puzzle which can be circumvented (by omission) if necessary. The essential analogy as far as the translator is concerned is that which Tolkien the philologist creates between fictional languages and real ones. Within the device of the pseudotranslation, the persona of the 'editor' now merges with that of the 'translator' to explain how the different languages of the text-world have been rendered in such a way as to make them comprehensible to the reader at the same time as retaining the original relationship between them. The literary reason for this is one of verisimilitude, as explained above. For a long time there was a convention in the English-speaking world that the speech of non-English characters in books or films is represented as heavily accented English, with a few interjections of *sacré bleu!* or *Schweinhund!* to establish the nationality. This is at best an unsophisticated solution, and indeed some film directors have experimented with original language dialogue interpreted by subtitles. For Tolkien as a professional philologist, the convention was unsatisfactory; it might do for the younger readership of *The Hobbit*, but it would be anomalous in the much more highly developed text-world of *The Lord of the Rings*. Therefore he established the 'fact' (and anchored it in the histories) that throughout the area in which the tale is set there was a *lingua franca* known as Westron, or the Common Speech, which within the framework of the pseudotranslation could be represented by English. In this way the invented languages which formed a part of his linguistic conception could stand out as exotic and help create a sense of cultural otherness.

But unfortunately (for the translator) this binary opposition is complicated by linguistic variations within the Common Speech. For example, in the text the Hobbits find that the language of Rohan seems to bear a similarity to their own language, but in a highly archaic form, so the 'editor/translator' chooses to reflect this relationship by that between modern English and Old English. The more northerly language of Dale (represented by the Dwarf-names), which is also more distantly related, is represented by Old Norse. The translator and critic should note (although the 'editor/translator' does not and cannot, since he is inside the text-world and therefore cannot comment on its workings) that the use of these older Germanic languages is an important constituent of the contrast between the modern and the archaic, heroic world which underlies Tolkien's calque, as explained in detail by Shippey (1992).

The information contained in this Appendix is of most relevance for translators in two areas: the explanation of variations in linguistic register and of the principles of nomenclature. The comments on register can be summarised as follows (since they paraphrase the 'editor/translator', they must be expressed from within the text-world):

1. The Common Speech has been translated entirely into English, while languages alien to it remain in their original form, denoting something linguistically and culturally exotic to the Hobbits, through whose eyes the events are mostly seen.
2. There were many variations in the Common Speech, which was used by different races over a wide geographical area. Most Hobbits spoke a rustic dialect, while in Gondor a more formal and conservative register was used. This has been reflected, although to a limited extent, by the use of different registers in English.
3. The Common Speech had a 'familiar/formal' distinction in the second person, which has sometimes, though not consistently, been shown in English by the use of the archaic *thou*.
4. The Hobbit dialect had lost this distinction and used only the familiar forms, which explains why they sometimes sounded unusually familiar in more formal situations.
5. More learned and widely travelled characters such as Frodo and (especially) Gandalf show a variation in style according to the company they are in.

The 'translator' notes that "Translation of this kind is, of course, usual because inevitable in any narrative dealing with the past" (Tolkien 1992:1168), which in text-world language is a reference to the conventions of representing foreign speech mentioned above, but adds that he intends to carry it further by applying it to names. The comments on nomenclature are more complex and detailed, but the main ideas are:

1. All names in the Common Speech are translated according to their sense.
2. A number of doublet forms appear, denoting that at the time of the story the names were extant both in the Common Speech and another language, usually Sindarin, one of the two Elvish languages, which functioned as 'cultural' languages analogous to Latin in the European Middle Ages.

3. Most of the Common Speech names were translations of the Sindarin ones, so the English translations often match the Sindarin at one remove, such as *Hoarwell* (*hoar* + *well* = "spring of greyish-white water" – AT) to represent *Mitheithel* (*mith* + *eithel*). Others took the form of folk-etymologies, such as Brandywine as a plausible corruption of *Baranduin*.
4. Such linguistic relationships between an unknown language and an English translation are necessary for the reader to appreciate the impressions of the Hobbits through whose eyes the events are seen, as in the course of their travels they experience some things and places which are familiar to them and their linguistic world, while others are wholly exotic.

This last point, to step back out of the text-world, holds the key to the use of language throughout the whole text, and indeed, following Shippey (1992:65), to the literary function of the Hobbits as mediators between the reader of today and the archaic, heroic world of *Beowulf* or the Norse sagas, the spirit of which some nowadays find hard to approach: the familiar set against the exotic. It is implicit throughout both *The Hobbit* and *The Lord of the Rings*, but it is at this point that Tolkien comes closest to expressing it within the metatext. So the device of pseudotranslation is intimately bound up with the way in which both the works (since *The Lord of the Rings* retrospectively draws *The Hobbit* into this device through the 'Red Book of Westmarch') gain their effect, rather than being just a conventional or playful conceit.

But it is point 1 which is of most immediate concern to translators. Since the Common Speech is represented by English, then in a translation it will be represented by the target language in order to maintain the linguistic relationships. It was because Tolkien found these relationships, particularly as exemplified in the names, essential to the literary effect of his text, and because he found them not observed in the earliest translations, that he decided to compile a set of notes to be made available by the publishers to future translators. After his death they were edited by his son Christopher and published as 'Guide to the Names in *The Lord of the Rings*' (Tolkien 1975). They are concerned exclusively with names formed from English elements, that is to say those which represent the Common Speech and which one would therefore expect to see translated into the target language. Since the structures of English nomenclature on which Tolkien based his own names are inseparable from the history of the language,

Tolkien considered that some philological information would help translators to understand the principles he was drawing upon. They form a real-world counterpart to the text-world Appendix F II, to which they refer as an essential source, but they provide what the metatext could not, namely an explanation of the author's (as opposed to the 'editor/translator''s) considerations in choosing particular linguistic forms.

4.6 Translation criticism and Tolkien's linguistic commentary

To conclude this long section, it is necessary to relate it all back to our model of translation. Stage B of Steiner's hermeneutic motion consists of an in-depth reading, an analysis of syntactic, semantic and ideological structures which ideally will include the complex literary and linguistic relationships detailed above. Since the translation is carried out within a prevailing critical and cultural framework, both the translator and the translation critic may make use of any existing critical commentaries, which may include other writings by the author if they are relevant. In the case of Tolkien, *The Hobbit*, *The Silmarillion*, the twelve volumes of *The History of Middle-earth* and the published letters may be used to clarify text-world references, while the linguistic texts Appendix F II and the 'Guide to the Names in *The Lord of the Rings*' can help to understand the machinery of the pseudotranslation, which is itself a constituent of the text-world.

But it is important to remember that any suggestions found here are justified for the translation critic not by any special status as 'authoritative' statements, but by the help they may give in preserving the integrity of the text-world as an essential component in the literary structure of the source text itself. Even if the Appendices are not included in the target text (since as we have seen, the metalinguistic commentary poses formidable problems for the translator), so that the reader is not explicitly made aware of how the nomenclature is constituted, it would mean a diminution of the artistic integrity of the work if the linguistic structure was not at least partially preserved in a form that is meaningful within the target language. How the translator decides which linguistic distinctions it is desirable, or even possible, to replicate in the target language will be the topic of the next section.

5 Stage C – Translation as a Decision-making Process

As we have seen, the translator is the essential mediator, the link between the source culture and the target culture. Stage C represents the actual linking process which takes the minute analysis of Stage B and attempts to map all the details as closely as possible onto the more or less different matrix of the target language and target culture. This is the point at which decision-making becomes crucial. Since different languages do not correspond exactly in their syntactic, semantic and ideological structures, translators are constantly having to decide on the best possible approximation. However detailed the analytical model that is applied to the source text, and however many social and cultural parameters it takes into account, it is unlikely to suggest one solution and one solution only in the target language. In particular, the greater the importance of the poetic function of language in a text, as opposed to pure information, the more there is likely to be a conflict between (a) conveying the precise denotation of the words, (b) reflecting something of the ambiguity of connotation, and (c) preserving the formal features of the source text, or at least transforming them into corresponding formal features in the target language. In Tolkien's case there is the additional complication that words and their significance need to be viewed not only against the background of the source and target languages, but also against that of the text-world.

An influential model can be found in Levý's article 'Translation as a Decision Process' (Levý 2000). In the first part of the article he suggests ways of deciding between synonyms and near-synonyms by constructing semantic hierarchies, which may also include socio-cultural levels. A decision conditioned by the analysis at a higher level will then determine the range of choices available at a lower level. He illustrates his model by an analysis of different English translations of a short poem by Christian Morgenstern, suggesting that where there is a conflict between establishing equivalence at different levels, the higher level of equivalence should take priority. The literal translation given in the diagram is perfectly adequate on the lowest level of the denotation of the words, but it is inadequate on the higher level of poetic effect; since the comic style is the most important feature, the wordplay (in this case, rhyme) which makes it amusing must take priority over the information content of the individual words.

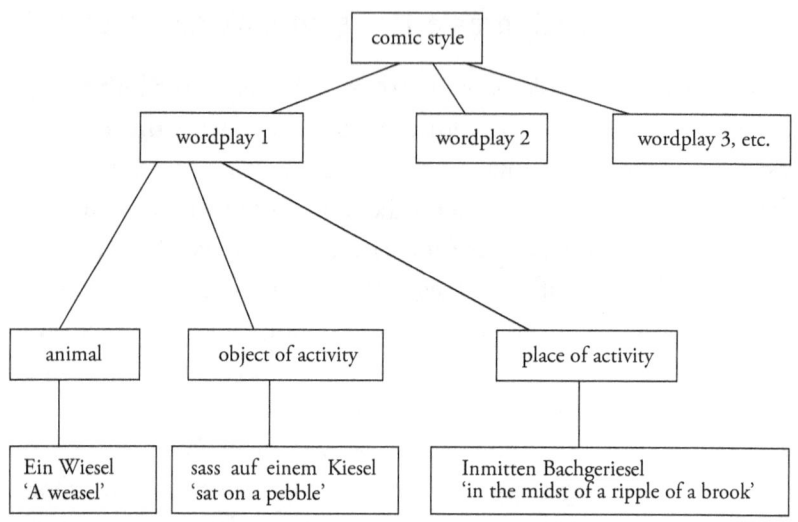

The solution is to change the individual words by substituting rhyming lexical items from potentially large paradigmatic sets of such items to occupy the positions 'animal', 'object of activity' and 'place of activity', which can be abstracted from the individual phrases. One version which keeps the subject of the sentence unchanged is "A weasel / perched on an easel / within a patch of teasel". However, Levý argues, it would be just as legitimate to substitute another animal, such as "A hyena / playing a concertina / in an arena", since what is important for the literary effect of the poem is not the precise meaning of the source text words, but the rhyming wordplay which contributes to an overall comic effect.

It must be said that the example represents a particularly clear case. It is a nonsense poem in which the informational content is minimal and the lexical items are chosen largely for their incongruity. But it would not be difficult to find a text in which meaning and form bear a more equal relationship, where the potential conflict would be more difficult to resolve. Nevertheless, Levý's model would seem to suggest that formal features should be privileged over individual meanings. To apply this principle to Tolkien is not easy, because although his style is often intensely poetic, offering denotation, a rich range of connotations, and a richness of sound effects such as alliteration and rhythm, nevertheless we are dealing not with a relatively short poem, but with a long and complex narrative, in which the precise details of events and descriptions are usually of major importance, so that if it is impossible to convey both denotation and aesthetic effect in the target language, the translator may choose to sacrifice the higher level. However, on occasions Tolkien introduces a sub-genre such as a song or a proverb, and here the translator may mark the difference by privileging the higher level as in Levý's model. For example, in Gandalf's song of Lórien in Meduseld, for the line "Unmarred, unstained are leaf and hand" the German translation substitutes "Schöner noch sind Laub und Hand", which is less precise in denotation and loses the text-world connotations of a realm preserved by Galadriel's ring from the effects of time, but which nevertheless keeps the smooth rhythm which is a feature of the source text. The French translation, on the other hand, remains faithful at the lexical level, but only at the cost of reducing this moment of incantatory stillness, immediately followed by Gandalf's *coup de foudre*, to mere lines of prose.

Levý's model does not offer a foolproof system, since in practice it is probably impossible to construct an *a priori* system to determine what is more or less important in literature. When it is applied to *The Lord of the Rings*, there may be considerable freedom and discussion over what should come at what level of the hierarchy, perhaps using different criteria to deal with different text passages. It might even be appropriate to take as the topmost level something like 'the text-world', since all the descriptions of people and places, all the Hobbit puns and proverbs, all the Gondorian ceremonies and Rohirric alliterative poems, the histories, the calendars and the writing systems only go to make up the vast, complex unity that is Middle-earth. The model will not yield a simplistic division into 'right' and 'wrong' translations, but that is not the point of the exercise. It may serve as a useful pattern in translation criticism if the critic can first try to discover the priorities that the translator has followed in making decisions of this kind and then present a reasoned challenge to them.

6 Conclusions: Proportion and Creativity

Now all four steps of Steiner's model have been presented and explained in some detail. It may be that potential critics feel the picture is not much clearer for them than it was before, or even less clear, which in a way may not be a bad thing, since it may discourage them from forming over-hasty and simplistic judgements. One thing that emerges is that there are a large number of conflicting demands placed on the translator, so it is important to keep a sense of proportion in any kind of criticism. So as not to seem unfair to the French translator in the matter of Gandalf's song above, it must be said that there is a good reason why he chooses to disregard the hierarchy at that point. French verse-form operates on completely different principles from that of English or German, being based on a fixed number of syllables rather than a regular alternation of stressed and unstressed syllables, and he evidently considered that to render the verses of *The Lord of the Rings* into a metrical form acceptable to French readers would involve too much re-casting of the denotations and poetic effects, even though it may seem a shame that the songs should be deprived of their inherent music. Levý allows for this by moderating the strict structure of the hierarchy with a principle known as *minimax*: the maximum effect for the minimum effort. This important escape clause recognises what has already been discussed under Stages A and D of Steiner's model: the translation has to be accepted by readers in the target culture.

Another (potential) example of its application concerns the use of second person pronouns. As we have seen, it is stated in Appendix F II that Westron had both familiar and formal forms, but the latter had dropped out of general use in the Hobbit dialect. To this, Tolkien adds the seemingly inconsequential remark that Pippin caused some astonishment on his first arrival in Minas Tirith by using the familiar forms to everyone, including Denethor. To achieve consistency between the text and the metatext, if this Appendix is included at all, translators into languages like German and French, which observe a familiar/formal distinction, should logically make Pippin use *du/tu* in their translations. But since nothing has come up in the text to prepare them for this anomalous usage, German and French readers would be likely to perceive this as an error of style by the translator, an impression which could be corrected only by a detailed footnote. Applying the principle of minimax, this involves a disproportionate effort both for the translator and reader to achieve a minimal gain. Fortunately, neither of these translations includes Appendix F II. The Italian translation, one of the few to do so, uses the familiar form throughout more frequently than the other two, so it is no surprise when Pippin says *tu* to Beregond and Bergil, and by the time Tolkien makes him address Denethor directly, he has presumably had time to learn Gondorian manners.

Of course, if ever a situation arose where, through some freak of reception, the one thing that the public knew about Peregrin Took was that he went around addressing people in a familiar manner, then translators would be perfectly justified in changing their personal pronouns accordingly. The importance of Stages A and D in our model is precisely that a consideration of the social and economic setting in which translations are produced moderates what might all too easily become a too rigid logical system in the other two stages. To repeat an important point, there is no perfect translation, and any solution is only provisional.

The Lord of the Rings contains a vast potential of significance for those who wish to study it closely, and this potential may not be entirely without effect for those whose chief concern is the story. In an ideal situation, the reader of a translation would be able to discover just as many levels as the reader of the source text. In concrete terms, that would mean that the whole network of linguistic relationships and their literary significance set up by the device of pseudotranslation would be accessible to the sensitive reader in the target language. But a 100% accurate replication of that network is impossible, because the structure is based on English, and each language holds a unique position within the family of related languages, which cannot be precisely replicated in any other target language, just as the nomenclature of England is uniquely linked to the topography and cultural history of England and cannot be mapped precisely onto any other location. Once again, each translator's solution is dependent upon time and place. The critic's task is to balance this solution against a reasoned assessment of what it is possible to achieve, rather than simply to condemn failure.

Although the emphasis throughout has been on exercising criticism based on clear principles, nevertheless scope must be allowed for the translator's creativity, unless translation is to be dismissed as a mechanical dictionary-dredging activity. In translating Tolkien, translators are forced to create, or at least to invent, in the frequent cases where Tolkien uses non-standard language: archaic lexis and syntax, or especially inventions of his own such as Germanic-style compounds (*sister-son*), re-creations from Old English (*mathom*), references to his own mythology (*silmarils*) and a large number of personal and place names, for which reference works will be of no use. All of these latter types are examples of original creation in the source language, so that the establishment of an equivalent in the target language will of necessity also be a creative act, even if it consists merely of utilising the source text term as a loan-word. Since so many of Tolkien's linguistic creations are derived from his professional knowledge of Germanic philology, translators into other Germanic languages may make use of historical analogies, but when the French translator produces the compound *fils-sœur* he has brought something original into the French language, and deserves recognition for that creative act.

Perhaps there is something valuable in the act of decision itself that is distinct from the perceived rightness or wrongness of the choice at the time when it is made. This is not peculiar to translation, but rather the need to make decisions constantly, based solely on the necessarily incomplete evidence before us, is an essential part of the human condition; it is both an aesthetic and a moral act, and emphasized as such just as much by Tolkien (for example, when Aragorn brings Éomer the "doom of choice") as by Sartre. It is expressed in poetic form by W. H. Auden, a onetime pupil of Tolkien and a vigorous advocate of his writing:

> The sense of danger must not disappear:
> The way is certainly both short and steep,
> However gradual it looks from here;
> Look if you like, but you will have to leap.
> (Auden 1966:200)

Even the best and most professional translators (or perhaps especially these) will have to leap on many occasions, although they will at least take the plunge only after weighing up the alternatives and their respective claims as carefully as possible; as we have seen above, even systematic models such as that of Levý cannot give definitive answers, although they may help to clarify the choice. Translation critics certainly need to exercise their critical faculties keenly, like a well-honed sword, but perhaps they should also temper them with a measure of goodwill. Even a less than perfect solution to a problem of translation can be absorbed into the complex meanings of the work and play a role in determining the reception of Tolkien as a version that has become familiar to a whole national group of readers over the years passes through Stage D of Steiner's hermeneutic motion into the Music of the Ainur.

About the author

Allan Turner's interest in language was awakened in his early teens by reading *The Lord of the Rings*. After studying German, medieval studies and general linguistics, he was 'Lektor' in English for fourteen years at the Universities of Trier and Basel. At present he lives near Newcastle upon Tyne and is completing a Ph.D. on problems of translating the philological element in Tolkien.

References

AUDEN, W.H., *Collected Shorter Poems* 1927-1957, London: Faber and Faber, 1966.

BAKER, Mona (ed.), *Routledge Encyclopedia of Translation Studies*, London and New York: Routledge, 1998.

BROOKE-ROSE, Christine, *A Rhetoric of the Unreal*, Cambridge: Cambridge University Press, 1981.

EAGLETON, Terry, *Literary Theory*, Oxford: Basil Blackwell, 1983.

GUTT, Ernst-August, *Translation and Relevance: Cognition and Context* (2nd edition, 1st edition 1991), Manchester: St. Jerome, 2000.

HAMMOND, Wayne G. and Douglas A. Anderson, *J.R.R. Tolkien: A Descriptive Bibliography*, Winchester: St. Paul's Bibliographies / New Castle, Delaware: Oak Knoll Books, 1993.

JONES, F.R., 'The poet and the ambassador: communicating Mak Dizdar's 'Stone Sleeper'', In: *Translation and Literature*, Vol. 9, Part 1, (2000), 65-90.

LEFEVERE, André, 'Acculturating Bertolt Brecht', In: Bassnett, Susan and André Lefevere, *Constructing Cultures: Essays on Literary Translation*, Clevedon: Multilingual Matters, 1998, 109-22.

LEVÝ, Jiří, 'Translation as a Decision Process', In: Lawrence Venuti (ed.), *The Translation Studies Reader*, London and New York: Routledge, 2000, 148-59.

SHIPPEY, Thomas A., *The Road to Middle-earth*, (second edition), London: HarperCollins, 1992.

J.R.R. Tolkien: Author of the Century, London: HarperCollins, 2000.

STEINER, George, *After Babel: Aspects of language and translation*, (second edition, first edition 1973), Oxford and New York: OUP, 1998.

TOLKIEN, J.R.R., *Tree and Leaf*, London: George Allen and Unwin, 1964.

Sagan om Ringen, (14th paperback edition, first published 1959), trans. Åke Ohlmarks, Stockholm: Bokförlaget Pan Norstedts, 1967.

Der Herr der Ringe: Band I Die Gefährten, Band II Die zwei Türme, Band III Die Rückkehr des Königs, trans. Margaret Carroux and E.-M. von Freymann, Stuttgart: Klett-Cotta, 1972.

Le Seigneur des Anneaux, Tome I La Communauté de l'anneau, Tome II Les deux tours, Tome III Le retour du roi, trans. Francis Ledoux, Paris: Christian Bourgeois, 1972.

'Guide to the Names in *The Lord of the Rings*', In: Jared Lobdell (ed.), *A Tolkien Compass*, New York: Ballantine Books, 1975, reprinted 1980, 168-216.

The Letters of J.R.R. Tolkien, (edited by Humphrey Carpenter), London: George Allen and Unwin, 1981.

The Peoples of Middle-earth, Volume 12 of *The History of Middle-earth*, (edited by Christopher Tolkien), London: HarperCollins, 1996.

Der Herr der Ringe: Band I Die Gefährten, Band II Die zwei Türme, Band III Die Rückkehr des Königs, trans. Wolfgang Krege, Stuttgart: Klett-Cotta, 2000.

TOLKIEN, J.R.R and E.V. Gordon (eds.), *Sir Gawain and the Green Knight*, (second edition, ed. Norman Davis, 1st edition 1925), Oxford: OUP, 1967.

Nils Ivar Agøy

A Question of Style
On Translating *The Silmarillion* into Norwegian

Abstract

The main challenge in translating Tolkien's *The Silmarillion* lies in the author's use of archaisms as a deliberate and fully integrated style element. The article discusses the particular problems of transferring this archaic mode into contemporary Norwegian and describes how the translator attempted to solve these problems by 'constructing' an ancient-sounding language style especially for this book. Some other problems encountered in the translation process are also briefly discussed, including a few ambiguities and possible errors in the original.

> 'Translation it is that openeth the window, to let in the light; that breaketh the shell, that we may eat the kernel; that putteth aside the curtaine, that we may looke into the most Holy place; that remooveth the cover of the well, that we may come by the water.'
> (The Translators to the Reader, *King James Bible*, 1611.)

1 Introduction

Translating J.R.R. Tolkien can be a tricky business. Quite apart from the problems inherent in the text itself, there are the numerous and often well-informed readers, who can be counted on to find and point out the smallest of mistakes and debatable points, and also the author, whose views on translation were clear and whose demands were strict. He knew very well what he was talking about, working closely with translations for much of his professional life, constantly referring to the various conundrums of translation in his writings, and even publishing metrical renderings of such fiendishly difficult medieval works of poetry as *Sir Gawain and the Green Knight* and *Pearl*.

It is well known how the translators of *The Lord of the Rings* into Swedish and Dutch were taken to task in the 1950s, Tolkien declaring that no "alterations, major or minor, re-arrangements, or abridgements of this text will be approved by me – unless they proceed from myself or from direct consultation" (Tolkien 1981:249). When the hapless translator into Dutch had translated some of the English names, Tolkien furiously accused him of deliberately attempting to destroy the local colour, of "pulling to bits with very clumsy fingers a web that he has made only a very slight attempt to understand" and more in the same vein (Tolkien 1981:250). Later translators may well shudder to think how he would have dealt with those tampering with *The Silmarillion*, the cherished core of his great 'legendarium'. Of course, not all translators care much about readers or even authors, but in Tolkien's case, they probably cannot afford not to. Dissatisfaction with early translations has triggered re-translations of two major Tolkien titles (*The Hobbit* and *The Lord of the Rings*) in Norway alone, costing the publisher money (and prestige) and embarrassing the original translators.

In this article, I will concern myself with the challenges of translating *The Silmarillion*, drawing on experiences gained when working on a translation into Norwegian in the early 1990s.[1] These challenges are partly general problems facing anyone attempting to translate from the Middle-earth corpus. The translation should have the *same degree* of consistency with the rest of the entire corpus as the original (as Christopher Tolkien reminds us, *full* consistency is not to be looked for) – which means, of course, that you have to be familiar not only with the text to be translated, but with all the other Middle-earth writings as well. The translator should form an opinion regarding the exact position of his/her text in the long and complex development of Tolkien's legendarium, and pay due consideration to the varied sources which inspired him and which he may have wanted to allude to. When translating *The Silmarillion*, familiarity with, say, the *Eddas*, *Volsungasaga*, *Kalevala* and *Beowulf* is *de rigeur*, not to mention the Old Testament. Ideally, the translator should not only be an expert on everything Tolkien ever wrote, but also on European mythology, history, languages, culture and on Roman Catholic theology. Needless to say, I have never had the pleasure of meeting the ideal Tolkien translator.

---

[1] It is often to some extent disagreeable for a translator to comment on his or her own work. Difficulties may easily be exaggerated and their attempted solutions presented as 'better' than they really are, consciously or unconsciously. Recommending specific solutions may also be construed as implicit criticism of colleagues who have chosen otherwise. I can only state for the record that I have tried my best to remain constantly aware of the risks while writing this article on invitation.

The more the translator knows about Tolkien's legendarium, the more chastened he or she is likely to be. When you have seen how the texts have been changed and polished through numerous revisions and rewritings to give a carefully measured effect, you are not encouraged to take any liberties!

2 Characteristics of *The Silmarillion*

Translating *The Silmarillion* is largely a question of style. There are a few other problems and considerations, which will be briefly discussed later, but they are all small compared to the stylistic ones. Tolkien wrote of *The Lord of the Rings* in 1956 that "there are many special difficulties in this text. To mention one: there are a number of words not to be found in the dictionaries, or which require a knowledge of older English" (Tolkien 1981:249). This is the case for *The Silmarillion* as well. The language used in the bulk of the book is deliberately archaic, employing terms and expressions which have passed out of everyday use, and also using words in other senses than is usual today. When, for instance, we read about the Dagor Bragollach that "the hosts of Hithlum were driven back with great loss to the fortresses of Ered Wethrin, and these they hardly defended against the Orcs" (Tolkien 1977:152), *hardly* is not (several *Silmarillion* translations notwithstanding) used in the contemporary standard sense of 'barely', 'almost not' or even 'with difficulty'. Instead, Tolkien reverts to an older usage of the word, 'with energy, vigorously, forcibly, violently'; a sense stated to be obsolete by *The Oxford English Dictionary*, the most recent example given dating from 1818. And in *The Silmarillion*, 'to take one's leave' does not simply mean to depart or say goodbye, but is used in the much older sense of a person of lower rank making use of a specific permission from his/her superior to do something (e.g. Tolkien 1977: 20, 135). Easy to miss – and actually missed in more than one translation.

The language of *The Silmarillion* is sometimes compared to that in the King James Bible of 1611, which, because of its almost unrivalled position until the early 20th century and its strong position even after that, has served to preserve many old words and expressions in the English language. The comparison is not entirely fair, the style of *The Silmarillion* is younger than the original *King*

James Bible, and it is uneven, but with all the 'thees' and 'thous' and 'dosts' and 'hadsts' one sees the point.

Why is the archaic style a problem? *Is* it a problem? Well, it should be noted that the potential problem does not lie in the language as such. If *The Silmarillion* had actually been written in 'King James English' in the 17th century, there would have been no difficulty. A translator would then render the language, representative of its period, as the contemporary version of the language he or she is translating to, just as Shakespeare's or Ibsen's plays are routinely translated into the current, modern versions of non-English and non-Norwegian languages, even if British and Norwegian schoolchildren read the originals and perceive them as hopelessly old-fashioned and sometimes incomprehensible. This is because neither Shakespeare nor Ibsen wished (with some exceptions) to write in an archaic mode. Tolkien, on the other hand, used his archaisms as a calculated style element.[2] These are therefore an integral part of the book. As such, they need to be translated. Taking the easy way out, translating *The Silmarillion* into standard contemporary language (yes, it has been done) would therefore mean that the translator chose to omit an important formal characteristic of the book. It would constitute an act of disloyalty to the author and of disrespect to the readers.

Other characteristics are the terse and laconic, sometime even monotonous style and the chains of sentences bound together with 'and', 'then', 'but', and 'now'. The book is supposed to be the final result of an extremely ancient tradition, where everything superfluous has been honed away by countless retellings down through the years.

Many native English-speakers find *The Silmarillion* hard to read. This is only partly connected to the language style, but has much to do with Tolkien's

---

2 He never, for obvious chronological reasons, commented on the use of archaic language in the published *Silmarillion*, but see his defence of archaisms (NB: intelligible archaisms) in *The Lord of the Rings* in Tolkien (1981:225f. – a draft to an unsent letter). He argues that old ways of speaking go with old ways of thinking; that people who think like King Théoden "just do not talk a modern idiom", and that to use modern language to represent Théoden's utterances would constitute "an insincerity of thought, a disunion of word and meaning". He goes on to state that 'heroic' scenes like Théoden's arming of Aragorn, Legolas and Gimli in Book III, Chapter 6, which he had described in old-fashioned language, simply "do not occur in a modern setting to which a modern idiom belongs". He seems to be saying that some things just cannot be expressed adequately in contemporary language – a point of view with which many will disagree, but which his translators should, in my opinion, respect.

use of an older way of telling stories and histories, deriving from societies ignorant of the Modern Novel, with its character developments, its psychology and motive analysis. Parts of *The Silmarillion* should be read in the way an Old Norse family saga was supposed to be read (or rather listened to), where Fate is a potent force, where characters act as representatives of families or clans, and where actions are supposed to be understood without explanation. Important events or facts are not always accentuated in the way we are used to, but are important all the same. The reader is expected not to forget that character A's great-grandfather inadvertently insulted character B's great-great-grandfather's brother, or exactly how character C is related to character D. Such a way of writing is rather unfamiliar to many readers, and has undoubtedly contributed to the book's reputation as remote and inaccessible.[3] It should, however, be noted that it does not permeate all parts of the book. The narrator of *The Silmarillion* often addresses us, as readers/listeners, as if he/she were omniscient – knowing the thoughts and counsels of the Valar, ascribing secret motives to human and elvish characters and so on. He/she speaks to us with the authority of someone who knows most of the answers. These passages are often more reminiscent of religious texts and/or of modern 'mainstream' novels than of medieval sagas. Sprinkled throughout the book is also a quite modern way of using adjectives, coupled with a peculiar predilection for describing almost anything relating to persons, their thoughts and feelings metaphorically in terms of their *hearts*. *Heart* is used more than 150 times in the 'Quenta Silmarillion' alone and is above all others Tolkien's word for all occasions. Hearts may be filled with this or that, they can overflow, be bound to objects, seek, rejoice, rest, be anxious, be torn, become clouded, turn hither or thither, be kindled, burn, cool, take colour and much besides. Literal-minded readers may even conclude that they are equipped with eyes![4]

The variations in the speed and manner of presentation, which no doubt has contributed significantly to *The Silmarillion*'s reputation as a 'difficult' book,

---

[3] Cf. Tom Shippey's commentary on *The Silmarillion* in chapter 7 of *The Road to Middle-earth*, particularly pp. 220-225 and pp. 238-240.
[4] "Wisdom was in the words of the Elven-king, and the hearts grew wiser that hearkened to him; for the things of which he sang, of the making of Arda, and the bliss of Aman beyond the shadows of the Sea, came as clear visions before their eyes" (Tolkien 1977:140). Using 'heart' in the sense 'person' is not very unusual (cf. 'sweetheart' and the like), but it is unusual to do it so often.

are of course partly explained by the book's character as an edited compilation from a large number of posthumous manuscripts, "a compendium in fact and not only in theory" (Christopher Tolkien in Tolkien 1977:8).

3 *The Silmarillion* in Norwegian – 'Inventing a Language'

When I accepted, in 1992, the task of translating *The Silmarillion*, my aim was to produce a text that would give, as far as possible, the same kind of 'feel' and connotations as the original and that would at the same time seem old and flow naturally. The text should, I thought, be taken seriously as purporting to be the end result of an authentic and extremely old tradition. It should in fact be treated as if the Tengwar manuscript had been dug up in someone's garden, i.e. none of the details which could shed light on the cultures and events it described should be adapted for stylistic purposes or the like.[5] And it should read as a translation, albeit a curiously archaic-sounding one, of the original Tengwar manuscript, not as a translation from English. (All the while, of course, respecting it as a work of art written in English and drawing on that language's resources.)

The main difficulty in trying to translate *The Silmarillion* into Norwegian was finding a suitable style of Norwegian to translate into. This is because the linguistic situation in Norway is fundamentally different from that of Great Britain. Norway has no literary language that would correspond even loosely to the one Tolkien used in the book, being at the same time dignified, austere, old and intelligible to the general reading public. The literary language used in the 18th and most of the 19th century was flowery and intricate, increasingly hard to understand for non-specialists, and is perceived today as stilted and generally associated with Danish. Indeed, it often was almost pure Danish. It is strongly linked in many peoples' minds with the Dano-Norwegian political union (1536-1814), which is still largely seen as a period of national humiliation. This also means that it is not associated with medieval times, but with the Renaissance and later periods. Trying to use it to describe 'medieval' conditions would seem

---

5 This may sound naïve. All translation must entail some loss or change of meaning. In practise, my principles were 1) Maximum (because 'total' is impossible) loyalty to the text; and, subordinate to this, 2) Maximum loyalty to the context (in this case both Tolkien's sub-created Middle-earth and the realities of Tolkien's own life). Cf. Nordahl (1991:48).

contrived in the extreme, unless indeed if one sought a mock-medieval, comic effect. The language(s) actually used before Danish was introduced (mainly Old Norse and Middle Norwegian) are totally incomprehensible to the average Norwegian today.

Then there is the fact that English has many more old loanwords than Norwegian. English has long ago naturalized many words of Greek, Latin and French origin that only found their way into Norwegian much later, if at all. This is both because the philosophical, political and material culture in the medieval and early modern periods was very different in Great Britain as opposed to Norway, and because the tiny Norwegian elites often made do with Latin, German and French. As a result, many words that can be used without any discord in *The Silmarillion* would stick out as unmistakeably modern and foreign in Norwegian. Examples are 'lieutenant' (Middle French/Latin), 'captain' (do.), 'demon' (Greek/Latin), 'myriad' (Greek), 'phalanx' (Greek), and 'signal' (French/Latin). Or try to imagine having to rewrite 'The Music of the Ainur' without ever using the Greek-derived 'theme'! All of these words can be used without any problem in contemporary Norwegian, but they would simply not have appeared in any Norwegian text hailing from the Middle Ages or earlier.[6]

In this situation and after much deliberation, I decided to try and construct a language style that would evoke the same reactions in Norwegian readers as I believed Tolkien had intended that his language should evoke in native English-speaking readers. For this to work, it was of paramount importance that the construction should not be perceived as such; it had to feel and sound natural and ancient.

My main strategies were:
- I strictly avoided using words that would be perceived as 'modern' or 'foreign', *even if* they happened to be the correct technical terms. When in doubt, I asked myself, 'If a Norwegian wanted to say this in the Middle Ages, how would he/she have said it – and how would a nationalist poet have rendered it in the 19th century?'

---

6 This is of course only a variation on the classic translator's dilemma: the *lingua a qua* always has different resources from the *lingua ad quam*.

- I frequently used words and expressions that 1) were old-fashioned or even obsolete, but which would be intelligible because they appeared in widely-known books, songs, poems or the like; and/or 2) referred to or evoked events or conditions in the mythical past, in antiquity or in the early or high Middle Ages. I was very concerned to use expressions that would seem familiar to the reader in some way, if only because he/she had had to read them at school and only dimly understood them. Into this web of allusions and indirect references were spun medieval ballads (surviving in oral tradition up to the 19th century), old Bible translations, fairy tales, hymns, historical fiction, the Norse saga literature, translations of classical epics such as the *Odyssey* and so on. In this work of trying to awaken half-forgotten expressions from slumber, I was luckily able to draw on the language in Nobel laureate and medievalist (and Catholic, inspired by such Tolkien-relevant figures as G.K. Chesterton and Dorothy L. Sayers) Sigrid Undset's novels set in Norway in the 13th and 14th centuries. I could also profit from the fact that Snorri Sturluson's 13th century *History of the Kings of Norway* is quite well known, and that most teenagers have to read at least one Norse family saga and parts of the Eddic poems in school. In many cases, a saga-like atmosphere could be created by very simple means, such as choosing one word order over another, or choosing words that, although fully understandable, are almost exclusively encountered in the sagas or fiction set in the Middle Ages. Some examples are 'måg' (*son/brother-in-law*), 'mannebot' (*recompense for a slain relative, wer(e)gild*), 'stormann' (*lord, noble, chieftain*), 'fylking' (*host, phalanx*), 'trell' (*slave, thrall*), and 'frende' (*kin*). I was of course fortunate to have this particular store of words to emphasize the fundamental (but not all-encompassing) cultural and conceptual correspondence between the saga universe and the First Age. On the other hand, I did not feel that I had any mandate to take a further step, and use kennings (the often highly standardized figurative phrases much used in Old Norse poetry, such as 'wave-horse' for 'ship', 'sword-storm' for 'battle' or 'ring-giver' for 'king'). Such paraphrases would ascribe to the peoples in *The Silmarillion* detailed cultural characteristics that they were not necessarily meant to have. One very rare exception was the use – once only, and in a descriptive passage – of 'blåmyrens vidder' [*expanses of the blue-mire*] to translate 'the deep ocean'.

The kenning 'blåmyren' is very firmly established as a synonym for the sea, and is associated with both sagas and fairy-tales.

- I chose moderately conservative forms (there is much leeway in Norwegian), but otherwise conformed to modern grammar and spelling. A particular problem was posed by the fact that some important words are today always spelt with diphthongs, which is generally a mark of 'low' or informal language. The most important were 'øy' (*island, isle*) and 'møy' (*maiden*), where the older 'ø' and 'mø' come over today not as archaic, but as stuffy, jarring and 19th century. I finally chose to use 'øy' through¬out, as it is a common word and occurred frequently in the text, but decided that 'mø' was acceptable if used very sparingly and only in titles such as 'Tåremøen' (*Tear-maiden*) and 'Alvemøen' (*Elf-maiden*). In such juxtapositions it acquired chivalric overtones.

- I insisted on using wholly obsolete forms of formal address ('I'/'Eder') to make possible several levels of formality. Using the rapidly vanishing 'De/Dem' (see above) would only have seemed bourgeois, while 'I'/'Eder' figures both in much-read historical fiction (e.g. in Undset) and in the 1930 Bible, although it has not been used in speech for well over a century, and even then only in very formal settings. I also insisted, in Tolkien's spirit, on using some words in senses deemed obsolete today, but tried to use them only where the context made the meaning clear. The publishers at one point queried my tentative resurrection of 'snekke' to translate *vessel* (of the Teleri ships put to fire by Fëanor), because 'snekke' is today almost exclusively used with reference to boats between 5 and 9 metres long, typically fishing vessels. However, 'snekke' was retained.

- In the 'Note on Pronunciation', the Index and the Appendix, I tried where appropriate to treat Elvish in its different forms as the original language, not English. This meant, among other things, using Norwegian and not English examples in the 'Note…', and finding Norwegian terms that would as far as possible cover all nuances in the *Elvish* word elements, not only the English translations, in the Appendix. It also meant, somewhat paradoxically, that the Quenya plurals *Noldor, Vanyar, Teleri, Valar* and so on could not be used directly, because of the way definite forms of nouns are constructed in Norwegian, with enclitic definite article (e.g. *the Noldor* became 'noldoene' in Norwegian, formed on the basis of the Quenya singular. Using 'noldorene' would have given the erroneous impression that the singular form was 'noldor'. Using 'noldor' without the enclitic '-ene' would have made it indefinite.) To avoid any loss of information, the Quenya plural forms were provided in the Index.

How successful these strategies were is, of course, not for me to say, but the translation has been well received.

4 Other Problems

I encountered relatively few translation problems apart from the stylistic ones. Some corrections could be made on the basis of *The History of Middle-earth* and other post-Silmarillion works, most notably revisions to the line of Númenorean kings. I firmly believe that "*beneath* the sheer walls of the mountains and the cold dark sea" in the description of Avathar (Tolkien 1977:73; my italics) should read '*between* …'. And however much I tried, I was unable to understand this sentence on p. 89: "For between the land of Aman that in the north curved eastward, and the east-shores of Endor (which is Middle-earth) that bore westward, there was a narrow strait". The description is clear and unambiguous, it appears in almost exactly the same words in 'The Annals of Aman' in *Morgoth's Ring* (Tolkien 1993:118), so it is not simply a misprint or a slip of the pen. It is even geographically possible – barely. The problem is that it does not at all agree with any other account of what the northern areas looked like. It is the *west* coast of Middle-earth that bears westward to the east coast of Aman. Or so I still think.

Some concepts were difficult because they have no exact or even approximate equivalent in Norwegian. *Quest* is perhaps the prime example. Then there were the numerous occasions where words containing 'mann' (*man*) had to be carefully (and hopefully undetectably) avoided because the people in question were not human. The alternative was to use them as unobtrusively as possible. I decided, for instance, that I could only make very sparing use of the standard word for *crew*, 'mannskap', if it referred to elvenships; and that the medieval-sounding and etymologically correct 'høvedsmann' for *captain* should not be used at all if the host was not human (the word was used instead to translate some less frequent words like *warden* and *chief*). The saga-like 'merkesmann' for *banner-bearer* was used, even for Eönwë, because 'fanebærer' came over as simply too modern and bland. 'Trollmann' for *wizard* was one of several unavoidables.

It is a standard saying among translators that you have never really read a book until you have translated it. Something I had not been prepared for in *The Silmarillion* was the number of ambiguities. When reading the original, I had admired what I perceived to be the simple, yet flexible style, which in spite of some lengthy sentences always seemed clear and unambiguous. When forced to consider every detail, I soon learned that there were far more possible interpretations and obscurities than I had reckoned with. Most were unproblematic. When, for instance, the text states that Morgoth set Húrin free of his captivity so that Húrin "should still further his hatred for Elves and Men, ere he died" (Tolkien 1977:227), it seems obvious to me that this refers to *Morgoth's* hatred, although at least one other European translation takes it to mean *Húrin's* hatred, which is of course *grammatically* possible. Others were more problematic, such as the description of how Húrin is left standing alone at the end of Nirnaeth Arnoediad: "Then he cast aside his shield, and wielded an axe two-handed; and it is sung that the axe smoked in the black blood of the troll-guard of Gothmog until it withered". Many readers will unconsciously choose an interpretation of this without considering that the last part of the sentence is ambiguous. Was it Húrin's axe that withered, as we can read in at least one published translation, or was it Gothmog's troll-guard? None of the alternatives are obvious. That the axe smoked in blood does not necessarily mean more than that the struggle was hard, but then again we have indications that the black blood of the Dark Lord's servants may be corrosive. Glaurung's blood burns Túrin's hand, and when Frodo in a later age stabs the cave-troll in Moria, black drops of blood fell "and smoked on the floor". On the other hand, the fact that Húrin is ultimately overcome by orcs, not trolls, seems to point to the reading that it is the troll-guard that withers, as does the information that he "hewed off their arms" until the last. This would not be possible if the axe had been eaten away – unless of course we suppose that Húrin was able to change his weapon in the heat of the battle ... The parallel texts do not shed any light on the matter. I personally thought that the withering was all on the part of the troll-guard, but also that it was best in this and similar cases to preserve the ambiguity. Sometimes this was difficult. Tolkien's text does not explain, for instance, what exactly the "flaming bolts" were that fell ruinous upon the lands when Beren and Lúthien fled from Thangorodrim (Tolkien 1977:182). They are probably not lightnings, as these are mentioned in the previous sentence. They *may* be molten lava or pieces of rock – this would be consonant with the fire and smoke belching forth from the mountain, evoking mental pictures of volcano eruptions. But they may also conceivably be some kind of manufactured missiles or projectiles, which is the basic meaning of 'bolt'. Morgoth is after all a Vala, not to be reduced to a force of nature. I was simply not able to find a Norwegian word covering all (or only these three) possible senses without prejudicing the reader.

5 Lessons to Learn?

This article is primarily a personal testimony concerning one particular translation. By its nature it is hardly a useful basis on which to draw general conclusions regarding translation or even Tolkien translation. But if I may continue the testimony: I am profoundly glad that I accepted the task only after having worked with Tolkien's writings for many years, and in a situation where I was able to do the translation as a labour of love. In the Middle-earth books, the interconnections are so frequent and complex, and the pitfalls for the translator who does not know the larger structure so numerous and well hidden, that 'ordinary' competence and conscientiousness are simply not enough. I write this as someone who has fallen into enough 'translator's pitfalls' to last me a lifetime.

About the author

Nils Ivar Agøy, b. 1959, dr. philos., cand. philol. & theol., is Associate Professor of Modern History at Telemark University College, Bø i Telemark, Norway. He has, apart from historical works, written extensively on Tolkienian subjects and was co-founder of The Tolkien Society of Norway. He translated *The Silmarillion* (Silmarillion, 1994, awarded the Norwegian Association of Literary Translators' prize for best literary translation 1995); *Unfinished Tales* (*Ufullendte fortellinger*, 1997), and *The Hobbit* (*Hobbiten*, 1997). His Tolkienian research interests focus on Tolkien and Christianity (he edited *Between Faith and Fiction: Tolkien and the Powers of His World*, 1998, Stockholm: Arda-sällskapet) an on Tolkien's sub-creation theory.

References

NORDAHL, Helge, 'Om å oversette et epos' ['On Translating an Epic'], In: Per Qvale, Bente Christensen, Gordon Hølmebakk and Solveig Schult Ulriksen (eds.), *Det umuliges kunst* [*The Art of the Impossible*], Oslo: Aschehoug, 1991, 46-57.

SHIPPEY, Tom A., *The Road to Middle-earth*, (second edition), London: HarperCollins, 1992.

TOLKIEN, J.R.R., *The Silmarillion*, (edited by Christopher Tolkien), London: Allen & Unwin, 1977.

The Letters of J.R.R. Tolkien, (edited by Humphrey Carpenter), London: George Allen and Unwin, 1981.

Morgoth's Ring, (edited by Christopher Tolkien), London: HarperCollins, 1993.

Vincent Ferré, Daniel Lauzon, David Riggs

Traduire Tolkien en Français: On the Translation of J.R.R. Tolkien's Works into French and their Reception in France

Abstract

This article first discusses the link between the history behind the French translations of J.R.R. Tolkien's works and the reception of his works in France, as well as Tokien's reputation among both the general French readership and the French media. In the second part, *The Lord of the Rings* comes into focus, as we examine the problems raised by the translation of Tolkien's unique style, his creations and his universe into French.

> It is [...] surely intelligible that an author, while still alive, should feel a deep and immediate concern in translation. And this one is, unfortunately, also a professional linguist, a pedantic don [...].
> (Letter to Allen & Unwin, April 1956, *Letters*, n°188)

> And therein lies the unrecapturable magic of ancient English verse for those who have ears to hear: profound feeling, and poignant vision, filled with the beauty and mortality of the world, are aroused by brief phrases, light touches, short words resounding like harp-strings sharply plucked.
> ('On translating *Beowulf*')

1 Introduction

The Lord of the Rings has so much in common with *Beowulf*, as is generally known, that any attempt to translate this book may seem presumptuous, given the depth of the reservations towards translation in general that J.R.R. Tolkien expresses in his 'Prefatory Remarks' to the 1940 revision by C. L. Wrenn of J. R. Clark Hall's *Beowulf and the Finnesburg Fragment:*[1] he cautions those who imagine they know a text – *Beowulf* in this case – after reading

---

1 These remarks have been reprinted as 'On Translating *Beowulf* in *The Monsters and the Critics and Other Essays* (Tolkien 1997:49-71).

only a translation, for a translation is to him merely "an aid to study" (Tolkien 1997:49, cf. 52, 53).

Many of the pitfalls he warns of in these acute and stimulating pages on translation apply to any target language – but French has several more that are unique. Most importantly, although the historical influence of French on modern English is unmistakable, much of the basic framework of Tolkien's work (place-names, character names, and made-up words) is drawn from the rich store of English's Germanic heritage which French does not share. Additionally, the chronological order in which Tolkien's books have (or have not yet) been translated into French has had an influence on the reception of his works as a whole.

As these lines are written, previously untranslated works (*The Homecoming of Beorhtnoth, Beorhthelm's Son*, 'Mythopoeia', *The Letters* and soon *The Lays of Beleriand*) or revisions of previously published texts (*The Father Christmas Letters, The Lord of the Rings*) are in the works. This article will combine general remarks on the literary reception of Tolkien's works in France with observations drawn from problems with the French translation of *The Lord of the Rings*.

2 Translation and Reception of Tolkien's Works

Tolkien was published quite late in French. *The Hobbit* was translated (by Francis Ledoux) twenty-two years after the Swedish version (1947) and twelve years after the German (1957), but also after the Dutch, Polish, Portuguese, Spanish and Japanese editions. The turning point was 1970, when Christian Bourgois published *Admirations*, a collection of critical articles by Jacques Bergier concerning texts by J. Buchan, A. Merritt, I. Efremov, S. Lem, R. E. Howard and other authors who were almost unknown to the French audience. Subsequently, Christian Bourgois asked J. Bergier's opinion on which of these works should be published first. He suggested four texts, one of which was *The Lord of the Rings*. To do the translation, Christian Bourgois chose Francis Ledoux, who had not only translated *The Hobbit*, but also a vast catalogue of works by Ch. Dickens, H. Fielding, D. Defoe, E. A. Poe, Horace Walpole, Ch. Williams, W. Shakespeare, H. Melville, Joyce Carol Oates, Tennessee Williams, etc. The first two volumes (*La Communauté de l'Anneau* and *Les deux Tours*) appeared two years later in 1972, with the final volume (*Le Retour du roi*) appearing the following year.

Christian Bourgois then began to make up for lost time by publishing *Leaf by Niggle* in 1974, shortly after the Dutch and Swedish versions (1971 and 1972).[2] Soon, the French translations were no longer lagging behind. When *The Adventures of Tom Bombadil* followed (1975), only the Swedish translation had been published first. Eventually, French translations of the posthumous books, namely *The Father Christmas Letters* (1976), *The Silmarillion* (1977) and *Unfinished Tales of Númenor and Middle-earth* (1980), came out with only a year or two of delay from their original publication in English.

French translations of Tolkien's works were produced during two main periods of intense editorial activity, namely the seventies (1969-1978) and from 1994 onwards:[3]

Bilbo le Hobbit (1969)	*The Hobbit* (1937)
Le Seigneur des Anneaux (1972-73)	*The Lord of the Rings* (1954-1955)
Faërie (1974)	Partial translation of *Tree and Leaf* (1964) and *Poems & Stories* (1980)
Les Aventures de Tom Bombadil (1975)	*The Adventures of Tom Bombadil* (1962)
Les Lettres du Père Noël (1977)	*The Father Christmas Letters* (1976)
Le Silmarillion (1978)	*The Silmarillion* (1977)
Contes et Légendes inachevés (1982)	*Unfinished Tales of Númenor and Middle-earth* (1980)
Peintures et aquarelles (1994)	*Pictures by J.R.R. Tolkien* (1979)
Le Livre des Contes perdus I et II (1995 and 1998)	*The Book of Lost Tales* (1983-84)
Roverandom (1999)	*Roverandom* (1998)

A new series of translations was begun in 1994, and the French versions of three recently translated works, Pictures by J.R.R. Tolkien (1994) and *The Book of Lost Tales, I and II* (1995 and 1998), deserve special attention, for they were

---

2 For the French edition, *Leaf* was bundled with 'On Fairy-Stories', *Farmer Giles of Ham* and *Smith of Wootton Major* under the collective title *Faërie*.
3 Chronological order – full references are given in the bibliography section.

translated by Adam Tolkien. This assures the French reader of a high quality of translation, even though few details are known concerning Adam's collaboration with his father, Christopher Tolkien, the editor of *The History of Middle-earth* series. Nevertheless, even if *The Homecoming of Beorhtnoth*, 'Mythopoeia', as well as the long-expected *Lays of Beleriand* and *Letters of J.R.R. Tolkien* are to be published in the coming months, many texts still remain unknown to the French readership – who often lack the skill to read Tolkien in his native language – and the fact that these 'missing texts' were not known has had a direct influence on the way Tolkien is perceived in France.

Indeed, most people in France are unaware that Tolkien's work stretches far beyond *The Lord of the Rings* and *The Hobbit*. The rest of *The History of Middle-earth* remains inaccessible to the average reader, as *The Book of Lost Tales* was seven years ago, and as *The Road goes ever on* or *Mr Bliss* still are. The French audience is presented with only a partial image and it is difficult to guess at the magnitude of Tolkien's cosmogony. Further exacerbating the problem is the fact that *The Silmarillion* is far less read in France than *The Lord of the Rings*, which itself was published for fifteen years without appendices.[4] Moreover, Tolkien's academic writings on medieval literature are totally unknown, even though '*Beowulf*: The Monsters and the Critics' was published almost thirty years ago in Swedish and German (Carpenter 2002:358).[5] The French audience has thus had no chance to see the link between his academic research and his fiction. This could have brought him well-deserved recognition in a country where Umberto Eco garners immense respect for his dual achievements.

Nevertheless, publication of *Le Seigneur des Anneaux* was warmly welcomed by some writers and scholars. It won the 1973 'Best Foreign Book Prize' (*Prix du meilleur livre étranger*) and J. Bergier even contemplated the possibility that J.R.R. Tolkien be awarded the Nobel Prize – provocatively suggesting that this would immediately spark vivid interest among French readers (Bergier 1970:173).[6] The most distinguished of these writers, Julien Gracq, mentions Tolkien in his well-known *En lisant en écrivant* (1980). He underlines the huge changes in the

---

[4] *The Appendices & Index* were eventually translated by Tina Jolas and published in 1986.
[5] Christian Bourgois Éditeur specializes in foreign fiction, which might explain why Tolkien's non-fictional writings have not been translated as a priority.
[6] J. Bergier was obviously extremely enthusiastic about *The Lord of the Rings*: at the end of his review, he praises American readers for being clever enough to read "this difficult book" (Bergier 1970:194).

contemporary literary canon, Tolkien having – to him – won full recognition, along with Simenon, as Dumas and Jules Verne had for the 19th Century (Gracq 1980:728, cf. 763, 619). More explicitly, asserting that he does not read much contemporary literature, J. Gracq makes an exception for Tolkien:

> My last very strong impression as a reader was due, seven or eight years ago, to *The Lord of the Rings*, by Tolkien: in this book, the virtue of the novel ['la vertu Romanesque'] reappears intact and new in a totally unexpected field. (Gracq 1986:1270, cf. 1269 on 'innocence')

In addition, Tolkien's name is to be found once more in a letter to the French review *Parages* in May 2001, when J. Gracq spontaneously evoked *The Lord of the Rings*'s 'achievement' ('succès') as a tale.[7]

In the academic field, Pierre Jourde published in 1991 the interesting *Géographies imaginaires* [*The Geography of Imaginary Lands*] on More, Gracq, Michaux and Tolkien, drawn from a PhD submitted in 1989. Three years before, Monique Chassagnol's impressive study addressed the question of *Fantasy in British Juvenile Stories* (1918-1968) [*La Fantaisie dans les récits pour la jeunesse en Grande-Bretagne de 1918 à 1968*]. But few PhDs have dealt with Tolkien: only ten between 1985 and 2001,[8] and one or two in progress. Similarly, only a few articles have yet been published on Tolkien,[9] and it was not before 2001 that the first French book specifically on *The Lord of the Rings* (*Tolkien. Sur les rivages de la Terre du Milieu*) appeared, while the translation (1981) of the excellent *Master of Middle-earth* by Kocher had been out of print for a long time.[10]

Is this lack of academic research to blame for the misconceptions of the media, who may otherwise rely on such research? Articles contemporary with the publication of *Le Seigneur des Anneaux* and, as it happened, with Tolkien's death are quite revealing of the French situation.[11] In September 1973, *Le Monde* reckoned that Tolkien "had remained unknown in France for a long time" despite the

---

7 Cf. http://www.parages.ens.fr/forum0.html (by courtesy of *Parages*).
8 According to the *Docthèse* database (July 2001).
9 Six of these articles, most of them written in the seventies, were republished in 1998 in a collection entitled *Tolkien en France* (Kloczko 1998).
10 Many readers had reservations about the one 'general' French book readily available on J.R.R. Tolkien (N. Bonnal, 1998, *Les Univers d'un magicien*).
11 *Le Monde* (September 5th 1973) is abridged as *M* 73, *Le Figaro* (July 22-23th 1978) as *F* 78, *Le Républicain Lorrain* (March 13th 1973) as *RL* 73, *Le Quotidien* (March 3rd 1983) as *Q* 83, *Lire* (March 2001) as *Lire* 01 and *Le Monde* (December 31st, 1982) as *M* 82.

publication of *Bilbo le Hobbit* in 1969, until *The Lord of the Rings* introduced him to a wider audience (*M* 73). Evidence of this lack of knowledge pervades the article, which introduces Frodo as Bilbo's son and Hobbits as 'small Elves'. Similarly, in the *Figaro*'s review of the *Silmarillion*'s French translation – which was very laudative, as was the *Républicain Lorrain* in evoking *The Lord of the Rings*'s 'spell' (*RL* 73) – the journalist felt the need to give a biographical sketch of Tolkien's life, as if it was unknown to the reader. This hardly seems to have changed ten years later when, in 1983, a paper in *Le Quotidien* supplied yet another biography and confused *The Hobbit* with *The Lord of the Rings*, as well as Dwarves with Hobbits.[12]

Almost from the beginning, Tolkien's work has been perceived by the media as an example of 'fantastique' and juvenile literature. First, it is worth noting that French has no equivalent for 'Fantasy' as a genre: the word is usually borrowed from English unless 'Fantaisie' is used, but may cause misinterpretation, for the word is equivalent to 'whim' or 'fancy' in contemporary French. In similar fashion, French journalists often use the adjective 'fantastique' to refer to 'Fantasy', which is a fatal misinterpretation, as Tzvetan Todorov has shown in underlining the important distinction between 'fantastique' and 'merveilleux' (Todorov 1976). *The Lord of the Rings* is definitely not a 'roman fantastique', but a romance in which 'merveilleux' is essential. Consequently, the link between Tolkien's work and our world is often overlooked by the media. The *Républicain Lorrain* was one of the first to assert, in 1973, that Middle-earth had come "from no-one knows where" (*RL* 73) – this long-lived misconception has surfaced over and over again.

Moreover, mainstream media have linked Fantasy with the juvenile, and stressed the picturesque elements ("Hobbits, a race of nice leprechauns," *RL* 73) to recommend *The Lord of the Rings* – and not only *The Hobbit* – to children. Lire even expressed a peculiar conception of juvenile literature in an article inviting the reader to "forget the overlong passages and slightly silly details" and to "bear in mind that you were once naïve" (*Lire* 01). One can find positive comparisons to Dumas and Proust, alongside such condescending statements,

---

12 According to *Le Quotidien*, in *The Lord of the Rings*, "The Hobbits go and find their ancestors' hoard, with Bilbo Baggins's help" (*Q* 83).

but that hardly seems to mend matters, for this kind of judgement did much harm to Tolkien's reputation in France.

Things took a turn for the worse as the French media evoked the possibility that Tolkien was a racist, basing this calumny mainly on the fact that he was born in South Africa and was 'conservative'. According to *Le Figaro*, Hobbits are extremely "reactionary," which "is indicative of the ideological slant of the work as a whole" (*F* 78) – but no evidence is provided to prove this – and *Le Monde* echoed an anonymous judgement of *The Lord of the Rings* as a "conservative utopia," because of the "rigidity of the society it describes" (*M* 82). Similarly, some Catholic magazines put an unreasonable amount of stress on Tolkien's religion[13] – although *La Vie* did publish an interesting and well-informed article in December 2001. And, finally, the French extreme-right sometimes refers to Tolkien's work for support, distorting his thought and writings.

But one has to ask if the French translation may (unwillingly) have given some weight to these misinterpretations – for instance by translating 'race' (of Dwarves, of Men, of Elves ...) by the literal 'race', which has a pejorative connotation in French. There were a few occasions when a translator of F. Ledoux's skill should have been more careful. For example, he uses 'noiraud' (*S* 94) to translate 'black-like' (*FR* 100),[14] an adjective used by the Gaffer in his description of a Black Rider. Ledoux uses the same term again (*S* 95) for 'a black chap' (*FR* 101) and (*S* 113 and 114) 'this black fellow' (*FR* 123 and 125). This is inexact, since the blackness refers only to the way the Black Rider is dressed (the Gaffer and Farmer Maggot could not have seen anything else), and it is unwarranted because it unnecessarily translates various English expressions by a sole French noun, and this is also dangerous because 'noiraud' refers to someone 'very dark-skinned or dark-haired' and is a synonym of 'moricaud', which is a racist term! The French translation should have been something similar to 'il était tout noir' or 'un type en noir', which both clearly refer only to his clothes. We are not saying

---

13 *Famille Chrétienne* published (in October 2000) a debatable article by Nicolas Bonnal, the same author of the extremely questionable *Les Univers d'un magicien*. The mistakes that pepper the article (the genesis of *The Lord of the Rings*, for instance, is supposed to have spanned the years 1946 to 1957) do little to recommend it.

14 *FR*, *TT* and *RK* refer to the three volumes of *The Lord of the Rings*, *S* to the French 'compact' edition (cf. bibliography). The book and chapter are indicated with Roman and Arab numbers, such as 'I, 2' for 'Book One, Chapter Two'.

that Ledoux was acting consciously, but rather that a translation, thirty years later, may, in another context (i.e. the rise of extreme-right in France), acquire a meaning which alters the original text and allows the possibility of grave misunderstandings. Evidently, there is an interaction between a book's translation and its reception, and rescuing Tolkien from the undeserved taint of racism would alone justify the undergoing revisions of many of Tolkien's works by Christian Bourgois Éditeur. There are, of course, many other problems to solve, and the current climate in France seems quite favorable for such a project.

When Peter Jackson's film adaptation of *The Lord of the Rings* was released, in December 2001, the French media – especially newspapers and magazines, including some as important as *Le Monde* (December 18th), *Télérama* (December 19th), *Les Inrockuptibles* (December 11th) or *Le Courrier international* (December 6th) – gave considerable attention to the book, inviting a French readership still largely unaware of Tolkien's existence to join the rapidly growing number of their compatriots who had read *The Lord of the Rings*. Sales figures for 2001 show that as many copies were bought in that single year in France as in the seven previous years combined (1994-2000). We may hope that an improved translation will give the French reader a more faithful rendering of Tolkien's works, and dispel the fabricated myth of this so-called 'racist writer of children's stories'.

Unfortunately (or fortunately for the purpose of this article), the French translation of *The Lord of the Rings* has been for many years the subject of virulent criticism, particularly on the Internet. Some convincing accounts of errors have been drawn up by critics both serious and dilettante, invariably unkind to Francis Ledoux. Yet it would be wise to remain careful and moderate, especially considering the difficulties that arise when one translates Tolkien's English, with all of its Anglo-Saxon sensibilities, into French – a language for which he had a notorious dislike.

3 Translating *The Lord of the Rings* into French

The Lord of the Rings presents some specific difficulties, such as the extreme need for consistency and coherence, the complexity of the invented world, the full use of the English language in its historical richness and wide vocabulary, as well as the abundance of allusions to older works of literature. The combination and sheer amount of these things make *The Lord of the Rings* uniquely difficult to translate.

Interestingly enough, a whole section of Appendix F is devoted to the matter of translation. This may come alternatively as a blessing or predicament to translators as it unveils a wealth of information but also introduces possible complications. In a particularly interesting passage, Tolkien describes a striking characteristic of hobbit-speech:

> The Westron tongue made in the pronouns of the second person (and often also in those of the third) a distinction, independent of number, between 'familiar' and 'deferential' forms. It was, however, one of the peculiarities of Shire-usage that the deferential forms had gone out of colloquial use. [...] Peregrin Took, for instance, in his first few days in Minas Tirith used the familiar for people of all ranks, including the Lord Denethor himself. (*RK* 515)

Tolkien remarks quite matter-of-factly that "this has proved impossible to represent"; and yet there arises the question of the opportunity (or desirability) of representing this in the French translation, where it is indeed possible (as is also the case with German, Spanish and indeed many other languages), 'tu' being the familiar form of the second person and 'vous' the deferential.

As tempting as it may be to hear Peregrin Took referring to the Lord Denethor as 'tu', one must bear in mind that this passage of Appendix F II is also part of the sub-creational process and is merely intended as a methodological account of the fictitious process of translation from Westron sources to English, not as a guide to eventual translators of *The Lord of the Rings*. Furthermore, any attempt to restore these distinctions between familiar and deferential would necessarily require arbitrary decisions on the part of the translator, for to this passage Tolkien adds as a footnote: "In one or two places an attempt has been made to hint at these distinctions by an inconsistent use of *thou*." But as this was not consistently applied, it is often difficult to be sure of Tolkien's intentions in his usage of the archaic English pronoun. Moreover, however clear Tolkien might have been on Shire-usage, consistent use of the familiar form of 'tu' in hobbit-speech, especially in the case of Sam addressing Frodo, would inevitably confront the reader with an extremely peculiar form of address not present in the original version of *The Lord of the Rings*, and potentially detracting from the author's true intentions in this matter.

But let us focus on facts specific to Tolkien's works: translating texts dealing with such a complex invented world as Middle-earth is indeed an undertaking of considerable proportions. Thirty years ago, before *The Silmarillion*, *Unfinished Tales* or *The History of Middle-earth* were published, the task was even more daunting. Nevertheless, this is what F. Ledoux, the French translator, undertook with *The Lord of the Rings*. Indeed, it proved impossible for the translator to fully grasp the richness of this universe, or sometimes to make the right decision concerning minute details of the underlying cosmology or mythology – although contrary to what has often been reported, Ledoux knew and studied the 'Guide to the Names in *The Lord of the Rings*' (published in *A Tolkien Compass* by J. Lobdell) and followed it for the most part. This can be easily demonstrated by examining key entries for which it is reasonable to assume that a translator, had he not read Tolkien's enlightening remarks, would most certainly have erred.

Good examples of this include the name 'Cotton', which bears no relation to the textile material despite the identical spelling, as well as other names such as 'Fallohide' that contain Old English elements, yet which were all correctly translated. Where the names are incorrectly translated, many were clearly chosen as the closest possible equivalents according to the Guide's indications, and only a few of them are actual errors on the part of Ledoux. It is worth reporting that F. Ledoux even told his publisher, Christian Bourgois, that he had written to J.R.R. Tolkien about the translation of such names as 'Bilbo', 'Frodo', etc., to justify his choices of 'Bilbo*n*' and 'Frodo*n*', which contradict the author's explicit instructions in Tolkien's 'Guide to the Names in *The Lord of the Rings*'.

But in spite of Ledoux's obvious care, many different kinds of errors did creep into his translation. The most famous (and horrendous) case of misinterpretation occurs at the end of the Prologue where "though Elrond had departed" and "the departure of Galadriel" (*FR* 21) are respectively translated as "bien qu'Elrond fût mort" ('though Elrond was dead', *S* 28) and "la mort de Galadriel" ('the death of Galadriel', *S* 28-29). Although this metaphorical usage is common in English – it is used in Book III, Chapter 1 ('The Departure of Boromir') – the translation as it stands is misleading and misinforms the reader about the fate of two important characters, and about the immortality (or rather 'serial longevity') of Elves. Another recurring mistake attributable to Ledoux's misconception of Tolkien's creation is the introduction of anachronisms or hints that can break the suspension of disbelief, whose importance Tolkien has underlined in his lecture 'On Fairy-Stories'. The first striking occurrence in the French translation is a reference to Brittany: when Frodo is described as Bilbo's "first *and* second cousin, once removed either way" (*FR* 29), Ledoux chooses "son oncle *à la mode de Bretagne*" (*S* 37), an expression used to indicate how intricate the family link is – a more correct translation would be "son cousin germain et cousin issu de germain, au deuxième degré des deux côtés." Ledoux runs equally afoul of 'single file' ("They went in single file along hedgerows and the borders of coppices ...," *FR* 94), translated by "Ils longèrent en file indienne" ('Indian file', *S* 89), although Ledoux does make a better choice in a later chapter ('à la file' for 'in a file').

In addition, we might examine the issue of prepositions, since it was apparently quite difficult to choose the right French ones for names such as Shire, Mordor, etc. For instance, Ledoux writes 'dans la Comté', and 'de Mordor', while French rules would command 'en Comté' (like 'en France', 'en Bretagne' or 'en Mayenne') and 'du Mordor'.[15] Apparently, the peculiar status of Middle-earth, which meant that no established usage could be referred to, bewildered a translator more used to Dickens' England. But since – to quote Tolkien's *Letters* – in Middle-earth "miles are miles, days are days, and weather is weather" (Tolkien 1995:272), why violate rules of grammar in places where the author makes no such violation, instead of simply transposing the existing rules to this invented world?

But one of the more ubiquitous mistakes is bringing in references to God or Christianity where the original text conspicuously omits them. 'Bless him', for example, is thus rendered by 'Dieu le bénisse' ("God bless him," *S* 37 cf. 126). Even in places without the slightest religious reference in the original, the problem surfaces in translation. The word 'cracker' (as in "not a single squib or cracker was forthcoming ...," *FR* 33) is translated as 'diablotin', an adequate equivalent but for its blatant etymological relation to 'le diable' ('the Devil'). Even worse, "[... if you don't keep your feet,] there is no knowing

---

15 Ledoux chose the masculine genre, thus 'Mordor' functions like 'Portugal' (for instance).

where you might be swept off to" (*FR* 99) is altered to "*Dieu* sait où tu pourrais être emporté" (*S* 92, emphasis mine), instead of 'nul ne sait où tu pourrais être emporté', for instance.

Purposeful repetition of a word or word group is one of many elements that influence the coherence of a work of literature. In his 'Prefatory remarks', Tolkien highlights the difficulties this can pose for a translator willing to be faithful to a text:

> No translation that aims at being readable in itself can [...] indicate all the possibilities or hints afforded by the text [Beowulf]. It is not possible, for instance, in translation always to represent a recurring word in the original by one given word. Yet the recurrence may be important. (Tolkien 1997:50)

This applies perfectly to *The Lord of the Rings*, where such repetitions (of single words or even of full sentences) are abundant and often essential to the understanding of the book. Some are obvious, such as in the case of the title of the initial chapter, 'A Long-expected Party' (*FR* 27) – which itself is a modified repetition of the title of the initial chapter of *The Hobbit* ('An Unexpected Party'). The expression 'expected' reappears in various forms throughout Book I: as an adjective ("there was a large crowd at Bag End, uninvited but not unexpected," *FR* 48, "a quite unexpected direction," *FR* 141), as a verb ("Expect me when you see me!" *FR* 53, "But I expected to find it," *FR* 74) and as an adverb ("coming unexpectedly after dusk," *FR* 60). Preservation of this recurring motif in the translated text is essential, since each repetition foreshadows ever more strongly the looming onset of Adventure.

An equally obvious example is Sam's almost literal quotation of Gandalf's advice: "he said *no! take someone as you can trust*" (*FR* 139) is the Samish version of "'But I don't think you need go alone. Not if you know of anyone you can trust, and who would be willing to go by your side [...]" (*FR* 83). Consequently, Ledoux's choice ("Emmenez quelqu'un en qui vous puissiez avoir confiance" (*S* 126) needs to be emended to '*Emmenez quelqu'un de confiance.*' This becomes all the more important as the repetition reveals itself as quite intricate, a cascading series of interconnected motifs: the adjective 'willing' is used again by Gildor in Book I, Chapter 3 – "'do not go alone. Take such friends as are trusty and willing'" (*FR* 112) –, whose advice is quoted (incompletely and indirectly) by

Frodo – "[…] even if they are willing to come" (*FR* 114) – and more explicitly by Sam – "Gildor said you should take them as was willing" (*FR* 139). Once more, Ledoux either failed to notice or chose to ignore this repetition, since he uses respectively 'disposés' (Gildor) and 'volontaire[s]' (twice, for Frodo and Sam)[16] – a better choice might have been 'determiné[s]', which fits in all three situations.

This 'foolish inconsistency' is too often a fault of the French translation. Such a commonly used and important noun as 'Ringwraiths' is translated in no less than three different ways: as 'Esprit servants de l'Anneau' (*S* 68 and 946), 'Spectres' (*S* 248), and even 'Chevaliers servants de l'Anneau' (*S* 1009). A similar inconsistency plagues the translation of the poems. Frodo thinks he might have invented 'The Road goes ever on and on' (the song he sings in Book I, Chapter 3), while Pippin recognizes it as one of Bilbo's (*FR* 97-98). Tolkien carefully plays on the difference between the two versions, since we have read these verses fifty pages earlier, as sung by Bilbo (*FR* 47), the two differing only by one word. Bilbo's "Pursuing it with eager feet" is replaced by Frodo's "Pursuing it with *weary* feet" (emphasis mine), which foreshadows the immensity of Frodo's burden. Unfortunately, the French version misses the point totally, since the second occurrence of the song is translated in such a way as to make it practically unrecognizable as a variant of the first[17] (cf. Ferré 2001:261, 281).

Repetition is not, of course, the only element of Tolkien's narrative coherence in *The Lord of the Rings*, where even the smallest detail may foreshadow important episodes, and every nuance is important. Thus, in the French version, the flowers of Bilbo's garden are not 'peeping in' at the windows (*FR* 33) but merely 'stick up over the windowsills' (i.e. "débordaient au bord des fenêtres," *S* 40). The slight personification is not translated.[18] This would hardly be a major error in itself – but Tolkien may have been gradually introducing the reader to the notion of a world in which plants are not the innocuously inanimate things they

---

[16] "[…] ne partez pas seul. Emmenez avec vous des amis qui soient sûrs et disposés à vous accompagner" (*S* 103), "même s'ils sont volontaires pour venir" (*S* 106), "Gildor a dit que vous devriez prendre qui serait volontaire" (*S* 126).
[17] The song appears a last time in Book VI, Chapter 6, modified by Bilbo as a sign of his decision to renounce Adventure: "Let others follow it who can!" (*RK* 321).
[18] Tolkien quite clearly chose very carefully (as usual) the terms in this sentence, as is revealed by a letter to Katherine Farrer (August 1954): "But *nasturtians* is deliberate, and represents a final triumph over the high-handed printers" (Tolkien 1995:183; cf. D.A. Anderson's 'Note to the text', *FR* ix).

are in ours, a process he continues on page 60 where he uses the metaphor of the 'fingers' of a tree (translated into French as simple 'branches'). Eventually we meet the mobile and forbidding trees of the Old Forest who "drop a branch, or stick a root out, or grasp at you with a long trailer" (*FR* 145), the terrifying Old Man Willow with his "sprawling branches going up like reaching arms with many long-fingered hands" (*FR* 154) and, of course, the Ents. Is Tolkien preparing us here for this journey away from the comfortable and familiar? It would hardly be the only occasion.

Many more instances of foreshadowing may be found early in the book, such as Frodo's first awareness of growing distant from his friends (a feeling which later increases significantly). During the farewell feast at Bag End he worries about the upcoming separation from Merry and Pippin required by his own plans: "The four younger hobbits were, however, in high spirits" (*FR* 90) the narrator notes. This is translated as "Les quatre jeunes Hobbits étaient toujours plein d'entrain" (*S* 86), where 'however' is rendered as 'still' and any sense of opposition between Frodo and his friends is dropped, as is the comparative 'younger' which places an implied emphasis on the age of an older Frodo. 'Old' is precisely the word Frodo chooses to describe himself a few pages later ("Be kind to a poor old hobbit!", *FR* 93), but is unwarrantedly scrapped by Ledoux ("Soyez bon pour un pauvre Hobbit!", *S* 89).

These nuances do not have to directly connect with other episodes in the book to be important. Although the book is written in third-person narration, Tolkien still occasionally adopts a Hobbit point-of-view by using subtle markers in his descriptions. For example, when the Black Rider forces Frodo, Sam and Pippin into hiding, the narrator's description tells us that "From inside the hood came a noise *as of* someone sniffing to catch an elusive scent; the head turned from side to side" (*FR* 99, emphasis mine). The Hobbits are baffled, they have no idea what this thing is that seems to be searching for them and so make a comparison to the familiar. But Ledoux's "le son de quelqu'un qui renifle ['a noise *of* someone sniffing'] pour saisir une odeur fugitive [...]" (*S* 93) is a mistake, because it makes concrete what was only metaphorical – especially since this device is used later again. In the same way, Tolkien's choice of where to use 'forest' and where to use 'wood' is not insignificant, even though Ledoux chose to consistently use the single French term 'forêt'. Where the Old Forest is instead referred to as a 'wood' we get a glimpse of the Hobbit's tendency to underestimate the place, since a 'wood' may evoke (to Hobbits) pleasant outings with friends, while a 'forest' is a much more wild and uncontrolled place – foreign to the calm and cultivated Shire.

The last quotations show Tolkien's careful use of the richness of the English language, which contains many more words than French. To quote a letter to Hugh Brogan, "Why deliberately ignore, refuse to use the wealth of English which leaves us a choice of styles[?]" (Tolkien 1995:226).

The variety of his vocabulary is striking, and sometimes difficult to match in French. For instance, a single word, 'iris', renders the English terms 'gladden' (the Gladden Fields) and 'iris', which explains a sentence like "to the Gladden Fields, where there were great beds of iris" (*FR* 70) being translated by "aux Champs aux Iris, où il y avait de grands parterres d'iris" (*S* 70). The French version sounds redundant, while in English the 'gladden' form, a variant of the dialectal 'gladdon', does not overlap with 'iris'. And Tolkien did specify, in the 'Guide to the Names in *The Lord of the Rings*' that translators should "avoid if possible" translating 'Gladden' by 'iris' (Tolkien 1975:185-186) – in addition to his 'Prefatory Remarks', in which he cautions that different (Anglo-Saxon) words should not be translated by a single one in Modern English (Tolkien 1997:56).

As if the extent of his vocabulary did not pose enough of a challenge for translators, Tolkien adds to it by coining neologisms. Leaving aside 'Hobbit', the most famous of his coinages, let us consider the word 'tweens', which designates, among Hobbits, "the irresponsible twenties between childhood and coming of age at thirty-three" (*FR* 28).[19] This term, reminiscent of 'twenties', 'teens' and 'between', is undertranslated by the French 'ses années intermédiaires' (*S* 35) or 'l'entre-deux-âges' (*S* 59), which clarify the 'betweenness' but lose the other meanings. Why not try to invent an appropriate neologism, like 'vingtescence', which combines 'vingt' (twenty) and 'adolescence'?

Tolkien's broad lexical variety, which includes these ancient, half-forgotten or even invented words is broadened still further by his use of a wide range of

---

19 *The New Shorter Oxford English Dictionary* gives two homonyms, "tween' (between) and 'Tween' (a "class of derivatives of fatty acid esters of sorbitan").

styles and dialects, from the high formality of Gandalf's or Elrond's speech to the idiolects of the Gaffer or Gollum. But what is broad in the original all too often becomes narrowed in the translation. A comparison of one of the Gaffer's dialogues to its translation serves to illustrate the problem:

> 'No, Mr Baggins has gone away. Went this morning, and my Sam went with him: anyway, all his stuff went. Yes, sold out and gone, I tell'ee. Why? Why's none of my business, or yours. Where to? That ain't no secret. He's moved to Bucklebury or some such place, away down yonder. Yes it is – a tidy way. I've never been so far myself; they're queer folk in Buckland. No, I can't give no message. Good night to you!' [The Gaffer, *FR* 92]

> Non, M. Sacquet est parti. Il est parti ce matin, et mon Sam est parti avec lui; de toute façon, ses affaires sont parties. Oui, vendues et liquidées, je vous dis. Pourquoi? Ça ne me regarde pas, ni vous non plus. Où? Ce n'est pas mon secret. Il est allé à Chateaubouc ou quelque part comme ça, au loin, là-bas. Oui, la route est bonne. Je n'ai jamais été aussi loin pour ma part; ce sont des gens bizarres, dans le Pays de Bouc. Non, je ne peux pas transmettre de message. Bonsoir! (*S* 88)

The French translation diminishes the peculiarities of Gaffer's speech, and even contains misinterpretations.[20] Similar observations could be made about Gollum's language: "'What had it got in its pocketses?' he said. 'It wouldn't say, no precious. Little cheat ... We ought to have squeezed it, yes precious ... precious!'" (*FR* 76) is prosaically rendered as "'Qu'avait-il dans ses poches?' disait-il. 'Je ne pouvais le dire, pas de trésor. Petite tricherie ... On aurait dû l'étouffer, oui, mon trésor... mon trésor!'" (*S* 74). 'Qu'*est-ce que ça* avait dans ses poche*ss*?' disait-il. '*Ça ne voulait* pas le dire, non, trésor. *Petit tricheur* ...' would be better (emphasis mine). For one may remember that Tolkien remarks, in the famous letter to Milton Waldman, that "even in style [*The Lord of the Rings*] is to include the colloquialism and vulgarity of Hobbits, poetry and the highest style of prose" (Tolkien 1995:159-160). And he insisted on the variety of speech, as he states in Appendix F:

> It will be noticed that Hobbits such as Frodo and other persons such as Gandalf and Aragorn, do not always use the same style. This is intentional. The more learned and able among the Hobbits [...] were quick to note and adopt the style of those whom

---

20 The 'secret' which 'ain't' one because everyone knows where Frodo has gone off to now becomes a secret that the Gaffer feels is not up to him to give away ('that isn't my secret').And the Gaffer's use of 'tidy way' indicates that, by the Gaffer's standards, it is a long way to Crickhollow (cf. 'away down yonder', 'so far'), not that it is *easy* to get there ('la route est bonne').

they met. It was in any case natural for much-travelled folk to speak more or less after the manner of those among whom they found themselves [...]. (*RK* 516)

Lastly, the variety of the vocabulary used in *The Lord of the Rings* is combined with an extremely acute awareness of the history of language. While reading this book, one cannot help thinking of Tolkien's remark on *Beowulf*'s lexis: "For many Old English poetical words there are (naturally) no precise modern equivalents of the same scope and tone: they come down to us bearing echoes of ancient days beyond the shadowing borders of Northern history" (Tolkien 1997:50). Since *The Lord of the Rings* was written in the 20th century, the case is different here, but the translator has to bear in mind that it is crucial to try and understand Tolkien's lexical and grammatical choices, and to reproduce them. This task is perhaps less daunting than it would be for a translation of *Beowulf*, since we can know if a particular term was archaic or rare at the time when *The Lord of the Rings* was composed (cf. Tolkien 1997:51). Tolkien explicitly addresses this issue in a letter to Allen & Unwin, when the question of translation (in Dutch) first arose. To him, "the assistance of the author" is essential, for *The Lord of the Rings* contains "many special difficulties," among which is the fact that "there are a number of words not to be found in the dictionaries, or which require a knowledge of older English" (Tolkien 1995:249).

Francis Ledoux is right, then, when he tries to give a similar impression of historical depth to the French reader by translating 'a pony-trap' (*FR* 53) by 'un tonneau à poney' (*S* 55) since 'tonneau' is rarely used with this meaning, and usually evokes a barrel; or again by translating "Why didn't I drive?" (Frodo, *FR* 96) by "Que n'ai-je pris une voiture?" (*S* 91). The reader (in 1972 and a fortiori in 2002) is sometimes obliged to modify his initial reaction to words. Taking into account the moment in history when the reading takes place is very important. This is confirmed by Tolkien (writing about *Beòwulf*): "The words chosen, however remote they may be from colloquial speech or ephemeral suggestions, must be words that remain in literary use [...] among educated people" (Tolkien 1997:55). Let us generalize, and say that the image of an 'ideal' reader (cf. Umberto Eco's analysis in *Lector in fabula*) must guide the translator. But anachronisms must be avoided: as in the borrowing of a 19th century English word to translate "In that room there are *three* tubs" (*FR* 133) by "Dans cette pièce, il y a *trois* tubs" (*S* 121).

It might even be argued that, in order to compensate for the extensive use of older, sometimes archaic or dialectal forms of English difficult to reproduce in French, the technique of borrowing (and calquing, in the case of word groups) has often been resorted to. Ledoux's gamble was to take advantage of the fact that a number of common English words were originally borrowed from Middle French. Some of these words survive in contemporary French, but their meaning may be slightly altered, the ancient meaning forgotten or found only in older literature. Ledoux's technique consists of using these words in the older sense, reborrowing them, as it were, from English. Following this plan from the start, Ledoux translates "they [...] delighted in parties" (*FR* 2) as "ils se plaisaient aux parties" (*S* 12) and "first hobbit to become famous" (*FR* 1) as "premier hobbit à devenir fameux" (*S* 11), whereas 'parties' and 'famous' would naturally translate as 'fêtes' and 'célèbre' in this context. Similarly, the very common English phrase 'a couple of', found in Book I, Chapter 9 ("a couple of dwarves," *FR* 204) is calqued in the French translation ("une couple de nains," *S* 178). This usage now seems archaic (and perhaps incomprehensible) in modern French, although it remains highly in favour in Quebecois French.

One of the areas where a sense of the depth of time can be most firmly established is in the choice of names (for characters and of places). Let us first remark that some names have, besides a purely historical depth, a connection with literary history, and take on additional resonances. Examples dating back to *The Hobbit* may be given, such as 'Beorn', which Tolkien explains as being an Anglo-Saxon term (Tolkien 1997:51); but they are much more abundant in *The Lord of the Rings*. To mention only one, 'hall' (in 'Brandy Hall' for instance) is full of echoes, and is, in particular, connected with *Beowulf*. As a consequence, Ledoux's translation by 'château' (castle) alters the reference and sounds too 'Arthurian' and 'grand'. Moreover, Ledoux uses the same noun to translate '-bury', in 'Bucklebury' (Chateaubouc) and 'Norbury' (Norchâteau). Since the 'Guide to the Names in *The Lord of the Rings*' indicates that the latter means '(fortified) town' (Tolkien 1975:190) and derives from the "Old English *burg*, mean[ing] a place occupying a defensive position, walled or enclosed; a town" (Tolkien 1975:180). A proper translation could be 'Fertébouc' and 'Norferté', respectively, the Old French 'ferté' meaning 'fortress, fortified town' and having survived in place-names – which has the added benefit of avoiding the use of 'bourg', used in the French 'Hobbitebourg' for 'Hobbiton'. As for 'hall', a comparison of three French translations of *Beowulf*[21] has not been very helpful, for the Anglo-Saxon term translated in English by 'mead-hall' is rendered in French by 'salle', 'grand-salle', but also 'palais'. Thus, it is necessary to use different translations following the context, 'grand-salle' (*S* 100) and even 'demeures' (*S* 101), and maybe 'Castel' for 'Brandy Hall' (Castel-Brande), which has the interest of consistency, since 'Woodhall' is already (rightly) translated by 'Castelbois' – but Grendel is no longer evoked for the French reader.

The 'Guide to the Names in *The Lord of the Rings*' indicates the origin of names, their meaning (when obscure or archaic, like 'Fallohide'), their consistency, and their mutual links. For instance, 'Shirriff' is supposed to be close to 'Shire' (Tolkien 1975:173), which is lost in Ledoux's choice of 'Shirriff' and 'la Comté'; but this case is rather difficult, since Tolkien gives two different suggestions:

> Since this word [*Shire*] is current in modern English and therefore is in the tale in the Common Speech, translate it by sense. (Tolkien 1975:191)

> Actually a now obsolete form of English *sheriff*, 'shire-officer,' used by me to make the connection with *Shire* plainer. In the story *Shirriff* and *Shire* are supposed to be special hobbit-words, not generally current in the Common Speech of the time, and so derived from their former language related to that of the Rohirrim. Since the word is not supposed to be Common Speech, but a local word, it is not necessary to translate it, or do more than accommodate its spelling to the style of the language of translation. It should, however, resemble in its first part whatever word is used to represent *Shire* (see this entry). (Tolkien 1975:173)

A choice has to be made, and it is more logical (and interesting) to treat them as 'Common Speech' words, and to translate them consistently. This decision is not too problematic, if we keep Ledoux's translation by the feminine 'la Comté', while 'Shire' would more normally be translated as 'le Comté'. It fits quite well the description that the word is "not generally current in the Common Speech of the time." The most important thing is the relation between 'Shire' and

---

21 *Beowulf*, edited and translated by A. Crépin (two volumes), Göppingen: Kümmerle, 1991; *Beowulf*, translated by J. Queval, Paris: Gallimard, 1981; *Beowulf*, translated by D. Renaud, Lausanne: L'Age d'homme, 1989.
Bilingual (Old English and Modern English) edition: *Beowulf*, edited and translated by M. Swanton, Manchester & New York: Manchester University Press, 1994.

'Shirriff'. Merely borrowing the latter in French is disastrous, for it irresistibly evokes Indians and the American Far West. The solution may be to use 'connétable'. It does not have *exactly* the same meaning (the word was used to designate the head of the French royal army), but seems more suitable since it is derived from *comes stabuli*, i.e. *'comte* de l'étable' or 'count of the stable', a position whose original responsibilities were not entirely dissimilar to those of the shirriff.

To suggest etymology, and the presence of words within words, we have also decided to amend Ledoux's decision to leave the Shire place-name of 'Rushey' untranslated (*FR* 130). Tolkien suggests that this name should be translated, meaning 'Rush-isle' (Tolkien 1975:190). The basis of the French translation must be 'jonc' (rush). But instead of using 'jonchaie', 'joncheraie', or 'jonchère' ('the place where rushes grow'), why not choose 'Joncquisle'? It complies with the information given in 'Guide to the Names in *The Lord of the Rings*' and attracts the reader's attention because although there is no actual etymological connection with 'jonquille' (daffodil), it does look like it, and it conspicuously contains 'jonc' and 'isle', an archaic spelling form for 'île' (island). This may be a way to invite an awareness that Tolkien's names have an etymology worth exploring, and that there is more about them than meets the eye – to paraphrase Gandalf's comment about Frodo (*FR* 430).

4 Conclusion

> [...] I suddenly realized that I am a *pure* philologist. I like history, and am moved by it, but its finest moments for me are those in which it throws light on words and names! (Tolkien 1995:264).

This review of the circumstances surrounding the French translations of J.R.R. Tolkien's works shows the strong link between the translations and the image the media and readers have of this writer. But we must keep in mind that the specific difficulties raised by the translation into French of Tolkien's writings can explain delays in publication (e.g. of *The History of Middle-earth*) as well as explain the rather incomplete success of Francis Ledoux's translation of *The Lord of the Rings* – though some of his more inspired translations, such as 'Fondcombe' for 'Rivendell', have delighted many French readers.

We hope that the revised edition of *Le Seigneur des Anneaux* will meet the expectations of the majority of the French readership when it is released. In any case, it is worth remembering Tolkien's words on translation:

> The effort to translate, or to improve a translation, is valuable, not so much for the version it produces, as for the understanding of the original which it awakes. (Tolkien 1997:53)

About the authors

Vincent Ferré teaches Comparative Literature at the Université de Rennes II (CELAM). His chief area of interest is the modern novel (1910-1950), especially Proust, Broch and Dos Passos. On J.R.R. Tolkien, he has published articles and *Sur les Rivages de la Terre du Milieu* (2001), an analysis of *The Lord of the Rings* which focuses on the theme of death. He has also been an advisor on the French translation of Peter Jackson's *The Fellowship of the Ring* and is in charge of translations of Tolkien's works for Christian Bourgois Éditeur.

Daniel Lauzon is majoring in Translation Studies at the University of Montreal. He is an avid reader and student of Tolkien's work and has discussed the film adaptation of *The Lord of the Rings* on his website *Elostirion*, which he created in 2000. He is currently revising the French edition of *The Lord of the Rings* together with David Riggs and Vincent Ferré.

David Riggs received his Bachelor of Arts degree in English literature from the University of Wisconsin, River Falls in 1991. His adventure began after innocently publishing a list of errors on a French Forum.

Works by J.R.R. Tolkien referred to in the article

TOLKIEN, J.R.R., 'Guide to the Names in *The Lord of the Rings*', In: J. Lobdell (ed.), *A Tolkien Compass*, La Salle: Open Court, 1975, 155-201.

The Letters of J.R.R. Tolkien, (second edition, first edition 1981, edited by H. Carpenter), London: HarperCollins, 1995.

The Monsters and the Critics and Other Essays, (paperback edition, first edition 1983, edited by Ch. Tolkien), London: HarperCollins, 1997.

The Lord of the Rings, (3 volumes, paperback edition, second edition 1966), London: HarperCollins, 1999.

French translations of Tolkien's works

The Hobbit: *Bilbo le Hobbit*, (first edition Stock, 1969), translated by F. Ledoux, Paris: Christian Bourgois, 1995.

The Lord of the Rings: *Le Seigneur des Anneaux*, (first edition 1972), translated by F. Ledoux, Paris: Christian Bourgois, 1995. [a revised edition is to be published in 2004]

The Book of Lost Tales: *Le Livre des Contes perdus*, edited by Ch. Tolkien, translated by A. Tolkien, Paris: Christian Bourgois, 1995 and 1998. [published in one volume in 2001]

Smith of Wootton Major, Leaf by Niggle, 'On Fairy-Stories', *Farmer Giles of Ham*: *Faërie*, (first edition 1974), translated by F. Ledoux, Paris: Christian Bourgois, 1996. [a new edition, revised and enlarged is to be published in 2003]

The Silmarillion and Unfinished Tales of Númenor and Middle-earth: *Le Silmarillion* (first edition 1978) followed by *Contes et légendes inachevés* (first edition 1982), edited by Ch. Tolkien, translated by P. Alien and T. Jolas, Paris: Christian Bourgois, 2002.

Pictures by J.R.R. Tolkien: *Peintures et aquarelles de J.R.R. Tolkien*, translated by A. Tolkien, Paris: Christian Bourgois, 1994.

Roverandom: *Roverandom*, edited by W.G. Hammond and C. Scull, translated by J. Georgel, Paris: Christian Bourgois, 1999.

The Lays of Beleriand: Les Lais du Beleriand, translated by E. Riot, Paris: Christian Bourgois. [to be published in 2003]

The Letters of J.R.R. Tolkien: Les Lettres de J.R.R. Tolkien, translated by D. Martin, Paris: Christian Bourgois. [to be published in 2004]

Selection of books (esp. in French) on Tolkien's works or mentioning him

BERGIER, J., *Admirations*, (second edition, first edition Christian Bourgois, 1970), Paris: l'Œil du Sphinx, 2000.

CARPENTER, H., *J.R.R. Tolkien, une biographie*, (second edition, first edition 1980), Paris: Christian Bourgois, 2002. [translation of *J.R.R. Tolkien – a Biography*, 1977]

CHASSAGNOL, M., *La Fantaisie dans les récits pour la jeunesse en Grande-Bretagne de 1918 à 1968*, Paris: Didier Erudition, 1986.

COUEGNAS, D. (ed.), *Les Cahiers de l'imaginaire. Dossier J.R.R. Tolkien*, Laillé: Société des Cahiers de l'Imaginaire, 1982.

DEVAUX, M. (ed.), *La Feuille de la Compagnie. Cahier d'études tolkieniennes*, Paris: L'Œil du Sphinx, 2001.

(transl.), 2001, 'J.R.R. Tolkien, lettre à Milton Waldman', In: *Conférence* 12, (2001), 714-56.

FERRÉ, V., *Tolkien. Sur les rivages de la Terre du Milieu*, (Paperback edition: Pocket 2002), Paris: Christian Bourgois, 2001.

GRACQ, J., *En lisant en écrivant*, 1980, and: 'Entretien avec Jean Carrière', 1986, In: Œuvres complètes II, édited by B. Boie, Paris: Gallimard, 1995, 553-768 and 1231-73.

HAMMOND, W.G., and C. SCULL, *J.R.R. Tolkien, artiste et illustrateur*, Paris: Christian Bourgois, 1996. [translation of *J.R.R. Tolkien, Artist and Illustrator*, 1995]

JOURDE, P., *Géographies imaginaires*, Paris: J. Corti, 1991.

KLOCZKO, E., *Les langues elfiques: dictionnaire quenya-français-anglais*, Toulon: Tamise productions, 1995.

(ed.), *Tolkien en France*, Argenteuil: Arda, 1998.

KOCHER, P., *Les Clés de l'œuvre de J.R.R. Tolkien*, Paris: Retz, 1981. [translation of *Master of Middle-earth: the Fiction of J.R.R Tolkien*, 1972]

LURIE, A., *Ne le dites pas aux grands, essai sur la littérature enfantine*, translated by M. Chassagnol, Paris: Rivages, 1991.

TODOROV, Tzvetan, *Introduction à la literature fantastique*, (second edition, first edition 1970), Paris, Seuil, 1976. English version: Todorov, Tzvetan, *The Fantastic: a Structural Approach to a Literary Genre*, translated by Richard Howard, with a foreword by Robert Scholes, Ithaca, N.Y.: Cornell University Press, 1975.

Sandra Bayona

Begging your pardon, Con el perdón de usted:
Some Socio-Linguistic Features in *The Lord of the Rings* in English and Spanish

Abstract

In *The Lord of the Rings*, the repeated occurrence of certain expressions in the characters' speech marks them as deeply as any other feature; thus, their speech idiosyncrasies become a fundamental part of their personality. Since its publication in 1954-55, Tolkien's epic has been translated into many languages, Spanish among them. Were these linguistic features retained in the translation? The purpose of this paper is to examine how the linguistic varieties are expressed in Spanish, to see if they help the readers who have not read the novel in the original language to perceive certain personal characteristics as depicted through speech.

1 Introduction

The question of the linguistic variation in the society in The Shire has already been looked into by Johannesson (1997) with interesting conclusions regarding the role of certain peculiarities in speech as marks of individuality and group membership. The purpose of this paper is to reflect on this issue once again, yet taking a different approach. The point of view will be that of a reader who has had access to the English version of *The Lord of the Rings* and to its translation into Spanish. It is the aim of this study to see how the linguistic variation mentioned above has been expressed in Spanish, and if the speech idiosyncrasies as part of the individual's character have been preserved. I would like to point out that neither the possibility of translation nor the methodology or the approach used in this particular instance will be under discussion. The focus will be rather on the question whether the translation enables the readers who have not read the novel in the original language to perceive the individual characteristics and the social differences as depicted through speech.

The material analysed comes mainly from the utterances of a specific group of hobbits comprising Sam, his father, and some of his friends. They are all members of the working class in The Shire. Occasionally, hobbits of the landed gentry are quoted, though the variation taken into account does not usually occur in their speech.

When the actual words of hobbits are quoted, the source is usually indicated by giving the speaker's identity (name), whereas the Roman numeral indicates the Book from which the quotation has been taken, and the Arabic numeral refers to the page.

All English quotations have been taken from the Ballantine Books edition of *The Lord of the Rings* (see bibliographical references), the Spanish translations from the Minotauro edition (see bibliographical references).

Although there has been a thorough search, it is possible that some instances of the structures studied have been overlooked. This does not mean they are not relevant and their absence must be blamed on human fallibility.

2 On Characterisation

In a first step, I will look at characters and characterisation and specifically consider the linguistic devices used in the original language (English) to characterise some of the protagonists. In a second step, I will analyse how these devices have been rendered into Spanish.

It is therefore necessary first to establish what is understood by *character*. According to Mieke Bal (1990), a character can be defined as a 'complete semantic unit'. This means that a character comprises a certain number of features that make him or her an individual and that allow the reader to distinguish him or her from the other protagonists in the story. These features may include a name, which usually lets us identify the subject as man or woman, a place of residence, activities carried out as part of his or her life, his or her social environment, his or her ideas on politics, society, sports etc. Sometimes a protagonist is defined by his or her physical features, sometimes by a psychological profile. The protagonist's position in a group or the relationship with other subjects in the story can also be defining. Each feature, then, opens up a number of possibilities while it closes down others.

As Bal points out, we, the readers, do not know much about the different characters when starting a book. We gradually come to know each protagonist as we advance in the story, aided by the description of their looks, behaviour and attitudes, their relationship with the others and the repeated appearance of certain features that we come to identify as fundamental traits of the protagonist's personality. The more marked and frequent a characteristic is, the clearer and more defined our idea of the protagonist's character becomes.

Tolkien uses various devices to construct the characters of the protagonists in *The Lord of the Rings*, and sometimes these elements enable the readers not only to identify the individual, but also his or her group-membership. The application of specific linguistic features, some of which can be considered as non-standard, is one of these devices and it plays a fundamental role in Tolkien's characterisation of his protagonists. By regularly allotting specific linguistic characteristics to the same individual, and to groups, Tolkien has led his readers to a better understanding and a more intricate knowledge of the creatures that live in Middle-earth.

3 Some Linguistic Features of Hobbits

Society in The Shire can be divided roughly into two groups. On the one hand, there are those who belong to the landed gentry, a sort of aristocracy, and who are often related to the Brandybucks and/or the Tooks. On the other hand, there are those who form the working class, which includes gardeners, farmers, and artisans and, one may add, also civil servants ('shirriffs'). We find several references to the existence of these two classes in *The Lord of the Rings*. There are comments on their daily activities, the protagonists themselves mention their own jobs, master-servant relationships are described, and the idiosyncratic speech variations reveal social positions within The Shire society.

If we pay close attention to the dialogues among hobbits (and sometimes to their exchanges with non-hobbits) we will notice that there are patterns used that do not conform to what is considered standard English, and that this variation coincides with the fact that the character who uses it belongs to the Shire working class.

However, this departure from the norm not only helps to reinforce class- or group-membership, but it also characterises the protagonists. To be more precise: the repeated occurrence of certain structures and expressions in the speech of an individual is as much part of a protagonist's personality as his or her physical appearance or moral traits. In other words, if one of these characters whose speech features numerous and frequent non-standard forms, spoke in a different way, then a very important part of their individuality would be lost.

What, then, are these features? I cannot list all of them,[1] but the following are typical for the speech of the lower-class hobbits: alteration of word order, duplication of the subject, replacement of standard verb forms for non-standard ones, and double negatives.

Besides this use of non-standard forms, the speech of some of the hobbits presents another peculiarity. As we read on and the story unfolds, we come across certain expressions that are typical of some of the protagonists, i.e. that enable the reader to recognise a specific individual in the story.

These expressions, in contrast to the ones mentioned before, are not grammatically deviant but in accordance with the rules of grammar. Yet, they do mark their users very clearly due to their repeated appearance in the utterances of the working-class hobbits. *And all, begging your pardon, I reckon, if you understand* are among the most frequent.

These two ways of linguistic characterisation (choice of non-standard forms and frequent use of a set of expressions) are part of the same strategy (linguistic variation). Tolkien used it not only to strengthen the individual character of each protagonist, but also to indicate group membership.

The following table (Table 1) provides a selection of non-standard forms used by hobbits. The corresponding translation into Spanish will be analysed later.

---

1 For a detailed account of non-standard forms used by hobbits, see Johannesson (1997).

Table 1

Form	Hobbit user
duplication of subject	Ham Gamgee (I, 43) Sam Gamgee (I, 104) Cotton (VI, 322)
double negatives	Ham Gamgee (I, 43) Sam Gamgee (I, 254; IV, 261; VI, 208) Hobbit beyond the gate (VI, 310) Hob Hayward (VI, 311) Cotton (VI, 320)
alteration in subject-verb agreement	Sam Gamgee (I, 104) Hob Hayward (VI, 309) Robin Smallburrow (VI, 313) Cotton (VI, 321) Young Tom Cotton (VI, 327)
sound elision	Maggot (I, 129) Sam (IV, 248) Robin Smallburrow (VI, 314) Cotton (VI, 322)
coinage	Ham Gamgee (I, 43) Several hobbits/voices (I, 43) Sam Gamgee (II, 477; IV, 341; VI, 314)

Table 2 shows the most frequently occurring expressions among those that are usually allotted to the working-class halflings.

Table 2

Expression	User
if you take my meaning	Sam Gamgee (II, 426)
if you know what I mean	Sam Gamgee (I, 90)
if you follow (me)	Ham Gamgee (I, 43) Sam Gamgee (I, 90)
if you understand (me)	Sam Gamgee (I, 118; I, 253; II, 426; IV, 311; IV, 340; VI 253; VI, 296; VI, 318)
I don't follow you	Sam Gamgee (I, 90)
I reckon	Sam Gamgee (reporting Ham Gamgee) (I, 104) Sam Gamgee (I, 44; I, 187; I, 223; II, 426; IV, 272; IV, 273; VI, 228; VI 240)
I don't reckon	Sam Gamgee (II, 426)
I('ll) bet	Sam Gamgee (IV, 29; IV, 250; VI, 257)
I('ll) warrant	Sam Gamgee (IV, 248; IV, 261; IV, 264; IV, 271)
I'll wager	Sam Gamgee (IV, 269)
I fancy	Sam Gamgee (II, 426; IV, 269; IV, 311; IV, 316; IV, 378; IV, 388)
begging your pardon	Sam Gamgee (I, 90; I, 138; I, 237; II, 474; II, 474; IV, 207; IV, 216; IV, 225; IV, 256; IV, 322; IV, 341; VI, 228) Ham Gamgee (VI, 327)
and all	Ted Sandyman (I, 45) Sam Gamgee (II, 362; II, 452; II, 478; IV, 300; IV, 341; IV, 383; IV, 403; IV, 403; VI, 208; VI, 234; VI, 290; VI, 300; VI, 307)

We can observe the following:
- the selected non-standard forms occur among lower-class hobbits
- the repeated use of specific (grammatically non-deviant) expressions is found, with few exceptions,[2] mainly among working-class hobbits

Concerning these expressions we notice that:
- they do not show any deviations from standard grammatical structures
- their frequency is relatively high in the speech of the working-class hobbits
- they can be grouped according to their function in the communicative situation
- expressions with similar meanings also share similar structures
- identical expression occur very frequently in the speech of one and the same hobbit and in that of working-class hobbits in general

The author thus uses linguistic variation as an important means for characterising his protagonists and the reader is enabled to differentiate between individual characters as well as between social groups.

4 Non-standard Forms and their Translation into Spanish

In a next step, then, I will discuss how the non-standard forms have been rendered in the Spanish translation. I will follow the sequence as given in Table 1.

The first item to be discussed is duplication of subject. Ham Gamgee, for example, converses with fellow hobbits in *The Ivy Bush* and says "*You see, Mr. Drogo, he married poor Miss Primula Brandybuck*" (I, 43; my emphasis). Ham Gamgee, Bilbo Baggin's gardener, uses the name of the person he is talking about and adds the personal pronoun immediately after the name. Since the pronoun should replace the given name, there is a redundancy of forms. Sam Gamgee, Cotton and Young Tom Cotton also duplicate the subject in their

---

[2] It should be noted that these variations do not appear in the speech of the landed hobbits, except for two cases: Pippin says "*and all that*" once (V, 55) and Bilbo, accommodating to Sam's speech, answers him by using an expression similar to the one just uttered by the young Gamgee: "*begging yours (your pardon)*" (I, 287).

utterances (cf., for example, I, 104; VI, 322; VI, 326). The Spanish translation makes Ham say "*Verán: el señor Drogo Ø se casó con la pobre señorita Prímula Brandigamo*" (I, 35)³

The translator has omitted the duplication so that the Spanish sentence is grammatically correct. If the duplication of subject had been rendered in Spanish, too, the sentence would have been grammatically deviant.

In the translation of the other instances given above, we observe that there is no duplication either.

Table 3

my dad, he says to me (I, 104)	mi padre Ø me dijo (I, 106)
your dad, Mr. Peregrin, he's never had no truck with this Lotho (VI, 322)	señor Peregrin, el padre de usted Ø nunca lo pudo tragar al tal Otho (VI, 384)⁴
Some of the Hobbiton folk, they saw it (VI, 326)	Alguna gente de Hobbiton Ø estaba allí y vio lo que pasó. (VI, 390)

However, in the second example, Farmer Cotton uses a structure that could be considered unusual, pointing to a peculiarity in his speech: instead of what would be the normal form to indicate possession in such a context, a different form is taken. Cotton says, *You see, your dad, Mr. Peregrin, he's never had no truck with this Lotho (VI, 322).* In Spanish the sentence is given as *Se da cuenta, señor Peregrin, el padre de usted nunca lo pudo tragar al tal Otho (VI, 384).*

The use of the phrase *el padre de usted* (*the father of yours*) instead of the more usual *su padre* (*your father*) has a double function. On the one hand, it avoids the ambiguity that *su padre* would create: if it had been *Se da cuenta, señor Peregrin, su padre nunca lo pudo tragar al tal Otho*, it could be interpreted that Farmer Cotton means Otho's father. On the other hand, it can be considered

---

3 My symbol; in this analysis, it is used to show that the structure in question has been omitted in the translation.
4 The name of the hobbit that Peregrin's father did not appreciate is given as *Lotho* in the English version, but as *Otho* in the Spanish translation.

an instance of linguistic variation used to individualise a protagonist, this time in Spanish.

Of the non-standard structures featuring verbs, two will be considered here: double negatives and subject-verb agreement.

The negative in English is formed by adding *not* immediately after the operator. Negative verb structures take compounds of *any*, affirmative structures take compounds of *no*. The determiners *either* and *neither* follow the rules for *any* and *no* respectively; *never* takes no other negator.[5]

Working-class Hobbits do not pay much attention to these rules, though. As can be seen in the examples below, they tend to apply negation in more than one way. Table 4 gives instances of double negation and their rendering into Spanish.

Table 4

Talking won't mend nothing (Sam. VI, 238)	Con hablar no remediamos nada (VI, 284)
It won't do no good talking that way (Hobbit. VI, 310)	No le hará bien a nadie hablando de esa manera (VI, 368)
I don't want to be neither (Sam. I, 254)	Ni lo uno ni lo otro (I, 281)
The Sackville-Bagginses won't never see the inside of Bag End now (Ham. I, 44)	Los Sacovilla-Bolsón nunca volverán a ver Bolsón Cerrado por dentro (I, 36)

The negation of the verb in Spanish does not take an auxiliary verb; it is formed with the adverb *no* (*not*) and other indicators of negation can co-occur with this adverb: *ninguno/ninguna, nada/nadie, ningún/ninguna*[6] (generally corresponding to compounds of *no/any* in English). The first example given above combines both the adverbial form *no* and the pronoun *nada*. This structure occurs also in the second sentence. The last two instances feature other elements also commonly used for negation: the conjunction *ni* (*neither/nor*) and the adverb *nunca* (*never*). Please note

---

5 See Close 1986. *A Reference Grammar for Students of English*, (ninth impression; first published 1975). Hong Kong: Longman Group Limited.
6 See Munguía Zatarain et al. (1998).

that the Spanish renderings of the English non-standard structures are all grammatically correct.

We have several examples in which hobbits deviate from the accepted standard of subject-verb agreement. In standard English, the Present Simple takes an inflected verb only with the Third Person Singular. Professor Tolkien made his upper class hobbits follow the norm, but he sometimes introduced a deviation from the standard form in the speech of the working-class hobbits. Here are some examples in English with the corresponding Spanish translation (Table 5).

Table 5

'Elves and dragons! I says to him (Ham Gamgee. I, 44)	*¡Elfos y dragones!*, le digo yo (I, 37)
What if you comes to a place where there's nowhere to put your feet or your hands? (Sam. VI, 251)	¿Y si cae en un lugar donde no haya nada en que apoyar los pies o las manos? (IV, 293)
They moves about and comes and goes (Cotton. VI, 321)	Andan siempre aquí y allá, yendo y viniendo (VI, 383)

The translation shows no deviation from the standard subject-verb agreement. This may be due to the fact that the system for the Simple Present in Spanish requires more forms than the two used in English (verb + ∅ or verb + -s), and so a possible combination in Spanish would hinder rather than help the reading process.

The same is true for sound elision, which is also a feature of the speech of working-class hobbits. Again, no instances of this deviant linguistic feature occur in the translation (see Table 6).

Table 6

They won't harm you – not unless I <u>tell'em</u> to. (Maggot. I, 124)	No les harán daño, a menos que yo lo ordene. (I, 128)
Swertings we <u>call'em</u> in our tales, and ride on oliphaunts, 'tis said, when they fight. (Sam. IV, 300)	Endrinos los llamamos en nuestras historias, y montan Olifantes cuando luchan, según dicen. (IV, 352)
And there's the Lockholes, as they <u>call'em</u> (…) (Cotton. VI, 322)	Y están las Celdas Agujeros, como ellos las llaman; (…) (VI, 383)
But I've a bone to pick with you, in a manner <u>o'speaking</u>, if I may make so bold (Ham. VI, 327)	Pero tenemos una cuentita pendiente, como quien dice, usted y yo, si me permite el atrevimiento (VI, 390)

Although sound elision is also a feature of non-standard Spanish, it has not been used in the translation. This may be due to the fact that sound elision in Spanish could not have been used on a one-to-one basis to render the English original. Yet, the device could have been applied in other instances so that sound elision would still occur as an element for individualising speakers.

The last category listed in Table 1 features forms that Tolkien coined to be used by his characters. This group comprises the noun *jools* (Ham), the verb forms *drownd* (Ham, Sam, several hobbits), *shirriffing* (Sam), and *trapessing* (Ham).

Jools appears as *joyas* (*jewels*; I, 36); the different forms of *drownd* have been translated as *ahogo* (*drown*; I, 35), *ahogándome* (*drowning*; II, 546), *ahogarse* (*drown*; IV, 403). Sam says "*Stop Shirriffing*" (VI, 314), which has been rendered as *abandonar el puesto* (*leave the job*; VI, 373).

Trapessing is an exception since it has been rendered as *medoreando* (VI, 390)[7], which is a coined word in Spanish. Compare *merodeando* (standard form) and *medoreando* (coined form). It is worth noting that this new term does not interfere with the reading process, and that it certainly marks Ham in the eyes of the reader.

To sum up, Tolkien uses non-standard elements and patterns of speech as a means to characterise his working-class hobbits. The Spanish translation, however, retains these features only very rarely. This may be due to the dif-

---

7 The term appears in the Spanish version in italics, which draws the reader's attention to its peculiar nature.

ficulties which such a transposition would pose. At any rate, the translator's 'correction' of the originally deviant forms does not alter the protagonists' characters beyond recognition, but they appear not as fully individualised as for the English reader.

5 Individualising Expressions and their Translation into Spanish

As it was noted before, non-standard forms are not the only means employed to individualise lower-class hobbits. We also encounter expressions used by these hobbits that are not grammatically deviant but which mark the users as much as other features. The key to characterisation lies here in the fact that an individual hobbit (or a group of hobbits) shows a preference for one peculiar expression which occurs frequently in his or her speech.

I will discuss the expressions as they appear in Table 2 above.

*if you take my meaning / if you know what I mean / if you follow me / I don't follow you / if you understand / if you understand me

The conversational function and general meaning of these expressions, which are most frequently used by Sam Gamgee (with one instance of Ham Gamgee), are very similar. They are employed to ensure that the interlocutor has grasped the meaning of what has been said. The most frequently occurring verb is *understand*, which is usually followed by an object. Table 7 gives an overview of the occurrence of the expressions.

Table 7

Expression	User	Occurrences
if you take my meaning	Sam	1
if you know what I mean	Sam	1
if you follow me	Ham - Sam	2
I don't follow you	Sam	1
if you understand	Sam	1
if you understand me	Sam	7

As becomes evident, these expressions are typical for Sam's conversational style.

Table 8 gives the translation of the expressions into Spanish.

Table 8

Expression in English	Spanish translation
if you take my meaning (II, 426)	si usted me entiende (II, 484)
if you know what I mean (I, 90)	usted me entiende (I, 90)
if you follow me (I, 43)	si ustedes me siguen (I, 43)
if you follow me (I, 90)	¿no ve usted? (I, 89)
I don't follow you (I, 90)	no lo entiendo (I, 90)
if you understand (VI, 253)	si entiende lo que quiero decir (VI, 253)
if you understand me (I, 118; II, 426; IV, 311; VI, 296)	si usted me entiende (I, 121; II, 484; IV, 365; VI, 352)
if you understand me (I, 253)	si se me entiende (I, 280)
if you understand me (IV, 340)	si me comprende usted (IV, 402)
if you understand me (VI, 218)	si me entiende (VI, 259)

If we analyse the information presented in this table, we can see that:
- the *if*-conditional has been kept in most of the cases
- *meaning* and *mean* have been translated into a form of the verb *entender* (understand) in both their occurrences
- *follow* (three occurrences) has been rendered in three different ways by means of forms of *seguir, ver, entender* (follow, see, understand)
- *understand* (eight occurrences) has been translated using *entender* (seven times) and its synonym *comprender* (once)
- forms of the verb *entender*, then, are the most frequent elements in the Spanish version of the hobbits' speech

Tolkien characterised the lower-class hobbits by having them use the same set expression(s) time and again. Yet, while an English expression occurs without or with only slight variation, the Spanish translation introduces variations that do not correspond to the originals. So it happens that two occurrences of one and the same word in English are translated by two quite different ones in Spanish.

This difference in treatment tends to obliterate the characters' typical way of speaking and, as a consequence, renders their personalities less distinct.

*reckon

Working-class hobbits also frequently use expressions with *reckon*. They are to be found mostly in the utterances of Sam (once when quoting his father, Ham), of Ham himself, of Hob Hayward, of Farmer Cotton, and of Robin Smallburrow. Table 9 gives an overview.

Table 9

Expression	User	Occurrences
I reckon	Sam (quoting Ham)	1
I reckon	Sam	7
I reckon	Ham	1
I reckon	Hob Hayward	1
I reckon	Robin Smallburrow	1
I reckon	Cotton	1
I don't reckon	Sam	1

Occurring both in the affirmative and the negative form, the expression is used to convey the speaker's attitude towards a proposition or idea. Table 10 provides the Spanish translations.

Table 10

Expression in English	Translation into Spanish
I reckon (I, 104; IV, 273)	creo (I, 106; IV, 318)
I reckon (I, 187)	digo (I, 202)
I reckon (I, 223)	tengo la impresión (I, 245)
I reckon (IV, 272; VI, 228; VI, 240)	me parece (IV, 317: VI, 271; VI, 286)
I reckon (I, 44)	reconozco (I, 36)
I reckon (II, 426)	diría (II, 484)
I reckon (VI, 311)	supongo (VI, 369)
I reckon (VI, 313)	∅ (VI, 372)
I reckon (VI, 322)	estimo (IV, 384)
I don't reckon (II, 426)	no creo (II, 485)

There are two points that are important with regard to the occurrence of this expression in English. First, it appears in the speech of many a lower-class halfling (compare the uses of *reckon* and those of *follow/understand*, etc.). Second, contrary to the expressions analysed before, there is no variation in the forms used. Out of this follows that this expression is not only typical of an individual, but marks a whole social group.

In the Spanish translation, then, things look different. Instead of using one and the same expression to render the English original, we find eight different verbs used to translate 13 occurrences of *reckon* and once the expression has even been omitted (shown as ∅ above). Although the Spanish words used to render *reckon* are all related in meaning to the English original, they nevertheless introduce shades of meaning that are not present in the original text. The Spanish translation fails to preserve the correlation between 'typical expression' and speaker, though it could have been done without problems. Thus, yet another character-building element has been lost in the translation.

*fancy

In the speech of working-class hobbits, expressions with *fancy* fulfil a role similar to the ones with *reckon*. Sam uses this expression to state his point of view.

Table 11

Expression	User	Occurrences
I fancy	Sam	5

The expression occurs only in the affirmative form and shows no variation in tense. Table 12 presents the corresponding items in Spanish.

Table 12

Expression in English	Translation into Spanish
I fancy (II, 426)	se me ocurre (II, 484)
I fancy (IV, 316)	imagino (IV, 372)
I fancy (IV, 378)	me parece (IV, 450)
I fancy (IV, 388)	∅ (IV, 460)
I fancy (IV, 311)	sospecho (IV, 365)

The Spanish translation again introduces variations not extant in the English original. Whereas we have five identical forms in English, the Spanish translation offers five different forms deriving from the verbs *ocurrir* (occur), *imaginar* (imagine), *parecer* (seem) and *sospechar* (suspect). Once the expression is omitted completely. The reader of the Spanish translation may notice that Sam tends to accompany his utterances by expressions belonging to the similar semantic field 'fancy', yet s/he will not recognise one particular expression as characteristic of Sam's speech.

*bet / wager / warrant

Another set of expressions that appears quite frequently comprises the verbs bet, *wager* and *warrant*. Again, as with *fancy* before, it is Sam who provides all the examples.

Table 13

Expression	User	Occurrences
I'll bet	Sam	1
I bet	Sam	2
I'll wager	Sam	1
I warrant	Sam	1
I'll warrant	Sam	3

As has been the case with the expressions containing *follow* and *understand* (see above), the expressions with *bet*, *wager* and *warrant* also share structure and meaning. The forms vary according to tense (present or future) and the speaker uses them to reinforce a point he has made before. Table 14 shows the Spanish translations.

Table 14

Expression in English	Translation into Spanish
I'll bet (IV, 250)	sin duda (IV, 291)
I bet (IV, 257; IV, 290)	Apuesto (IV, 299; IV, 340)
I'll wager (IV, 269)	no creo (IV, 313)
I warrant (IV, 248)	apuesto (IV, 308)
I'll warrant (IV, 248)	se lo aseguro (IV, 288)
I'll warrant (IV, 261)	apuesto (IV, 305)
I'll warrant (IV, 271)	eso se lo aseguro (IV, 316)

begging your pardon

Sam uses this expression very frequently. It also occurs in the speech of Ham and is used, though only once, by Bilbo.[8]

The meaning of the English originals have been preserved in the Spanish translation, yet again the translation introduces a variation of forms that has no equivalent in the original.

---

8 It should be noted that when Bilbo uses the expression, it is to accommodate to Sam's speech (cf. I, 287).

Table 15

Expression	User	Occurrences
begging your pardon	Sam	12
begging your pardon	Ham	1
begging yours	*Bilbo*	*1*

Since it is Sam who uses this expression most frequently, the reader will think of *begging your pardon* as typical of Sam's speech – maybe of the Gamgee family in general, though we have only one instance of its use by Sam's father. Table 16 provides the renderings into Spanish.

Table 16

Expression in English	Translation into Spanish
begging your pardon (I, 90; II, 474a)	Perdón (I, 89; II, 543a)
begging your pardon (I, 138)	¡Le pido perdón, (...)! (I, 145)
begging your pardon (I, 287)	con el perdón de ustedes (I, 321)
begging your pardon (II, 474b)	si usted me perdona (II, 543b)
begging your pardon (IV, 322)	Con perdón (IV, 379)
begging your pardon (IV, 256; IV, 341; VI, 207; VI, 216; VI, 225; VI, 228; VI, 327)	con el perdón de usted (IV, 293; IV, 403; VI, 247: VI, 256; VI, 268; VI, 271; VI, 391)
begging yours (I, 287)	*con tu perdón (I, 321)*

As in the examples before, the Spanish translation preserves the meaning of the original. *Begging your pardon* is applied in order to soothe the interlocutor, either for what has been previously said or done or for what is to come, and rendered in Spanish by the verb *perdonar* or the nominal form perdón. However, although no synonyms have been used, the Spanish text shows variation (five different renderings) whereas the thirteen English instances of *begging your pardon* are identical.[9]

---

9 It should also be pointed out that *con el perdón de usted* sounds strange (though not unnatural) for readers in Argentina; thus this particular translation succeeds in marking a character for the reader of the Spanish text in this country.

Begging your pardon, Con el perdón de usted 87

and all

The last expression to be discussed is *and all* which is used to round off a speaker's turn. Occurring most frequently in the speech of Sam (13 occurrences), it is also used by Sandyman (once) and by Pippin (in the form *and all that*) (see Table 17).

Table 17

Expression	User	Occurrences
and all	Sandyman	1
and all	Sam	13
and all that	Pippin	1

Table 18 provides the translations into Spanish.

Table 18

Expression in English	Translation into Spanish
and all (I, 45)	y todos (I, 37)
and all (II, 362; II, 478; IV, 383; IV, 403; IV, 403; VI, 208; VI, 300; VI, 307)	y todo lo demás (II, 409; II, 546; IV, 456; IV, 480; IV, 481; VI, 246; VI, 357; VI, 364)
and all (II, 452)	y lo demás (II, 515)
and all (IV, 290; IV, 300)	∅ (IV, 340; IV, 352)
and all (IV, 341)	y todo (IV, 403)
and all (VI, 234)	y a todos (VI, 278)
and all that (V, 35)	*y de todo el resto (V, 29)*

The most frequent form in the Spanish translation is *y todo lo demás*. The remaining instances are variations of this expression and *todo* and *demás* are also used alternatively. The variations with *todo* (all) link the utterance to the preceding words. The plural *todos* is chosen when the speaker has mentioned other characters or groups (cf. I, 45: the ones mentioned are the people of Middle-earth and Gandalf; in VI, 234, they are Sam's friends). The meaning, once again, is not altered, but different words have been taken to translate one and the same English expression and there are even occasions when *and all* has been omitted in the Spanish text. Although the semantic level is not affected by these changes, they obscure the fact that *and all* in the English text functions as a linguistic marker.

6 Non-Standard and Standard: Some Reflections

We have seen that it is often difficult to reproduce the same non-standard features in a translation. The question whether or not these elements of linguistic characterisation could be replaced by other linguistic elements remains outside the scope of this study.

The discussion of the expressions used (predominantly) by working-class hobbits has shown that they are not only in-group markers (i.e. identifying the speaker as belonging to the working class), but that they are also used as a means to individualise protagonists via their speech idiosyncrasies. These idiosyncrasies, then, can (and should) be reproduced in a Spanish translation and do not require a deviation from the grammatical norm (as would the rendering of non-standard forms). Yet, the current Spanish translation does not pay attention to the importance of these idiosyncrasies. Thus, an expression that can be considered typical of a speaker since it occurs frequently and in identical form, is either rendered by a variety of differing Spanish forms or even omitted.

So while the translator can make an excuse for not reproducing non-standard forms, (s)he cannot do so in the case of individual protagonists' speech idiosyncrasies.

7 Conclusion

My discussion has shown that the differences between the English original and the Spanish translation do not affect the unfolding of the plot, nor do they impinge on the reader's appreciation of the protagonists. The readers of the Spanish translation and the ones of the English original come to know the same people, witness the same events, with the identical outcome.

Yet, it must also be kept in mind that Tolkien's depiction of the speech of lower-class hobbits (as the group under discussion in this paper) provides a wealth of additional information. A reader is not only able to recognise a speaker's group- or class-membership, but his linguistic idiosyncrasies contribute to the reader's recognition of the protagonist's individualised character. If these typical speech elements are not reproduced in translation, then part of what makes each protagonist unique is lost.

As a consequence, we must criticise the Spanish translation's practice of obscuring or weakening the protagonists' typical characteristics of speech.

Do we, then, come to know the same hobbit as the reader of the original English text? – Yes, but to a lesser degree.

About the author

Sandra Mercedes Bayona graduated as Teacher of English at the Instituto de Enseñanza Superior and is a lecturer at the Universidad Autónoma de Entre Ríos and the Universidad Nacional de Entre Ríos. She has done research on different topics in the fields of English history, language and literature, and is currently working towards her degree in Modern Languages and Literature.

References

AITCHISON, Jean, *Linguistics*, (fourth edition; first published under the title *General Linguistics*, 1972), USA: NTC Publishing Group, 1993.

BAL, Mieke, *Teoría de la narrativa. (Una introducción a la narratología)*, (translated by Javier Franco), Madrid: Cátedra, 1990.

CLOSE, R.A., *A Reference Grammar for Students of English*, (ninth impression; first published 1975), Hong Kong: Longman Group Limited, 1986.

DURANTI, Alessandro, *Linguistic Anthropology*, (first published 1997), Cambridge, UK: Cambridge University Press, 1999.

JOHANNESSON, Nils-Lennart, 'The Speech of the Individual and of the Community in *The Lord of the Rings*', In: Peter Buchs and Thomas Honegger (eds.), *News from the Shire and Beyond – Studies on Tolkien*, Zurich and Berne: Walking Tree Publishers, 1997, 11-47.

Longman Dictionary of Contemporary English, Longman Group UK Limited, 1988.

Longman Dictionary of English Language and Culture, Longman Group UK Limited, 1992.

Longman Interactive English Dictionary, Longman Group UK Limited, 1993.

LYONS, John, *Language and Linguistics. An Introduction*, (first published 1981), Cambridge, U.K: Cambridge University Press, 1997.

MUNGUÍA ZATARAIN, Irma, Martha Elena Munguïa Zatarain y Gilda Rocha Romero, *Gramática de la Lengua Española*, México: Ediciones Larousse, 1998.

POZUELO YVANCOS, José María, *Teoría del lenguaje literario*, Madrid, España: Cátedra, Crítica y estudios literarios, 1994.

SPOLSKY, Bernard, *Sociolinguistics*, Hong Kong: Oxford University Press, 1998.

TOLKIEN, J.R.R., *The Lord of the Rings, Part I, The Fellowship of the Ring*, (first Ballantine Books edition, October 1965), New York: Ballantine Books, 1954.

The Lord of the Rings, Part II, The Two Towers, (first Ballantine Books edition, October 1965), New York: Ballantine Books, 1954.

The Lord of the Rings, Part III, The Return of the King, (first Ballantine Books edition, October 1965), New York: Ballantine Books, 1955.

El Señor de los Anillos. I. La Comunidad del Anillo. (translated from English by Luis Doménech. Original title: *The Lord of the Rings, I. The Fellowship of the Ring*, 1954), España: Ediciones Minotauro, 1991.

El Señor de los Anillos. II. Las dos Torres, (translated from English by Matilde Horne and Luis Doménech. Original title: *The Lord of the Rings, II. The Two Towers*, 1954), Buenos Aires: Ediciones Minotauro, 1985.

El Señor de los Anillos, III. El retorno del Rey, (translated from by English Matilde Horne and Luis Doménech. Original title: *The Lord of the Rings, III. The Return of the King*, 1955), España: Ediciones Minotauro, 1980.

Arden R. Smith

The Treatment of Names in Esperanto Translations of Tolkien's Works

Abstract

The Esperanto versions of *The Lord of the Rings* and *The Hobbit* are fairly typical translations of Tolkien's works. In the treatment of Tolkien's complex nomenclature, their translators have made use of the usual strategies, translating some names, modifying others, and leaving some in their original forms. This paper focuses on the methodology used by William Auld in *La Mastro de l' Ringoj*, pointing out the numerous inconsistencies in that translation. The nomenclature used by Christopher Gledhill and Don Harlow in their *Hobbit* translations is also compared and contrasted with Auld's renderings.

1 Intoduction

From 1995 to 1997, the firm of Sezonoj in Ekaterinburg, Russia, published the first translation of *The Lord of the Rings* into Esperanto, an artificial language created by L.L. Zamenhof in 1887 as a means of international communication. *La Kunularo de l' Ringo*, *La du turegoj*, and *La reveno de la Reĝo*, the three volumes of *La Mastro de l' Ringoj*, were translated by the noted Esperanto poet William Auld (Auld 1995, 1996, 1997). This was followed in 2000 by *La hobito, aŭ tien kaj reen*, a translation of *The Hobbit* by Christopher Gledhill, with poems translated by William Auld (Gledhill and Auld 2000). An excerpt from *The Hobbit* had also been published in Esperanto previously, namely Don Harlow's rendering of a portion of the twelfth chapter of what he called *La Hobbito* (Harlow 1991).

Because of the nature of Esperanto, native speakers of the language are few and far between, practically all of them being children of Esperantist parents with different mother tongues. All three translators of Tolkien into Esperanto are in fact native speakers of English, though all three have credentials in the world of Esperanto. William Auld has done great service to the Esperanto movement. He has written poems and textbooks, edited periodicals and anthologies, and translated poetry, plays, and novels.[1] He has been the editor of *The British Esperantist* for over a quarter of a century and has served as vice-president of the Universala Esperanto-Asocio (1977–80) and as president of the Akademio de Esperanto (1979–83). In 1998 he was named Esperantist of the Year and nominated for the Nobel Prize in Literature (biographical sketch in Gledhill and Auld 2000:2). Christopher J. Gledhill has been an Esperantist since 1985. He holds a doctorate in linguistics, in which field he has published numerous articles and books, including his 1998 work, *The Grammar of Esperanto: A Corpus-based Description* (biographical sketch in Gledhill and Auld 2000:2). Donald J. Harlow has written numerous articles, reviews, stories, and web pages in and about Esperanto, and has served as president of the Esperanto League for North America and as editor of its newsletter, *Esperanto U.S.A.*[2]

Although all three translators use similar strategies in translating the proper names in Tolkien's works, the following analysis will concentrate on Auld's treatment of the nomenclature of *The Lord of the Rings*. Gledhill and Harlow's translations will only be mentioned where they differ from Auld's, and discussion thereof will be postponed until Auld's translation strategies have been fully discussed.

A translator should have both a mastery of the language of the original and the ability to render it into the target language with both accuracy and style. Auld, being both a native speaker of English and a noted Esperanto translator and poet, is eminently qualified on both counts to translate *The Lord of the Rings*. His translation reflects this. His prose and poetry read well, flow smoothly, and generally capture the flavor of Tolkien's original. Despite a few infelicities, such as Auld's failure to recognize and render Tolkien's alliterative verse as such, the Esperanto version of *The Lord of the Rings* is in this respect a fine translation.

It is in the treatment of the proper names in *The Lord of the Rings*, however, that Auld's translation fails the test. Admittedly, Tolkien's system of nomenclature is perhaps the greatest obstacle for any translator of *The Lord of the Rings*.[3] It

---

[1] A bibliography of Auld's works from 1952 to 1998 appears in Cimpa 1999.
[2] A collection of Harlow's writings can be found on the World Wide Web at <http://www.webcom.com/donh/don/don.html>.
[3] Korĵenkov (1999:98–99) regards the "notora nom-problemo" (notorious name-problem) as one of the "kaptiloj" (traps) that await translators of *The Lord of the Rings*.

would be impossible for a translator to replicate the complex interplay between elements from English, Old English, Old Norse, Gothic, Celtic, and Tolkien's invented languages. For example, the English names should be interpretable to the reader, but if they are translated into another language, then their similarity to Old English forms used by the Rohirrim will be lost. If the Old English forms are likewise translated, then they will lose their special flavor. The question of whether to translate a name or to leave it unaltered is sometimes a difficult one, and frequently the translator has no other option than to choose the lesser of two evils.

2 The General Treatment

Auld treats the elements in the names in three different ways, either (a) translating them into Esperanto according to their meanings, (b) modifying them to conform with the orthography, phonology and/or morphology of Esperanto, or (c) giving them in their original forms. Every translator of *The Lord of the Rings* uses each of these strategies to some extent, though not in the same proportions.[4]

In general, those names that are in English and have readily interpretable meanings are translated into semantic equivalents (or near-equivalents) in the target language. Auld translates a large number of names in this manner, including the examples in (1).[5]

(1) *Apudakvo* 'Bywater' (I:36), *Arbobarbo* 'Treebeard' (II:72), *Boklando* 'Buckland' (I:21), *Bonkorpoj* 'Goodbodies' (I:47), *Bovblekulo* 'Bullroarer' (I:18), *Brandoboko* 'Brandybuck' (I:26), *Brandovino* 'Brandywine' (I:22), *Dikulo* 'Fatty' (I:140), *Grizaj Havenoj* 'Grey Havens' (I:24), *Grizinundo* 'Greyflood' (I:267; *Grizinindo* III:337 is a typographical error), *Kardolano* 'Thistlewool' (I:211)[6], *Kotono* 'Cotton' (III:267), *Kverkaŝildo* 'Oakenshield' (I:30), *Larvo* 'Maggot' (I:129), *Mornarbaro* 'Mirkwood' (I:20), *Neĝkolassjo*

---

4 Cf. Nagel's (1995) discussion of strategies employed in the German translation of *The Lord of the Rings*.
5 Page references are to the individual volumes of the Esperanto translation: I = Auld 1995; II = Auld 1996; III = Auld 1997. The abbreviation H refers to Gledhill and Auld's *La hobito* (2000).
6 If Auld had included the appendices or a more detailed map in his translation, this undoubtedly would have been his rendering of *Cardolan*, as well. See below.

'Snowmane' (II:153), *Okcidentajo* 'Westron' (I:21), *Okcidentio* 'Westernesse' (I:21), *Orhara* 'Goldilocks' (III:397), *Paĉjo Dupiedo* 'Daddy Twofoot' (I:39), *Provinco* 'Shire' (I:18), *Ruĝa Libro* 'Red Book' (I:17), *Subfusoj* 'Burrowses' (I:46), *Superulo* 'Thain' (I:22), *Vato* 'Gamgee' (I:38), *Vermlango* 'Wormtongue' (II:133), *Vesperstelo* 'Evenstar' (I:493), *Veterverto* 'Weathertop' (I:20).

In some instances, Auld's translations are inaccurate, as the examples in (2) demonstrate. Most of these errors could have been avoided, if Auld had consulted Tolkien's 'Guide to the Names in *The Lord of the Rings*' (Tolkien 1975).

(2) *Folikluzo* 'Leaflock' (II:89; *kluzo* 'lock (in a canal)'); *Mortigaj Marĉoj* 'Dead Marshes' (I:491; *mortigaj* 'death-causing'); *Printempo-rondo* 'Springle-ring' (I:48; *printempo* 'spring (season)'); *Rapidlumero* 'Quickbeam' (II:99; *lumero* 'beam of light'); *river' Elveno* 'Elven-river' (I:257; presumably interpreted as 'river named Elven' rather than 'Elvish river', though *elveno* means 'outcome' in Esperanto); *Transio* 'Staddle' (I:203; *trans* 'across', presumably because Auld interpreted the name as 'Straddle').

Auld's usual treatment of names that are not readily interpretable in English is to modify them to conform with Esperanto orthography, phonology and morphology. In most instances, this involves nothing more than the addition of a suffixed -*o*, which indicates that a word is a noun in Esperanto. Several examples of this sort of modification are shown in (3).

(3) *Adelardo* (I:59), *Anduino* (I:19), *Angmaro* (I:22), *Aragorno* (I:86), *Argelebo* (I:21), *Arnoro* (I:21), *Bag-Endo* (I:33), *balrogo* (I:433), *Bandobraso* (I:18), *Bankso* (III:347), *Baranduino* (I:21), *Barlimano* (I:201), *Belfalaso* (I:21), *Boromiro* (I:316), *Daerono* (I:421), *Dunlando* (I:20), *Elendilo* (I:27), *Elrondo* (I:32), *ento* (II:76), *Eorlo* (II:34), *Eriadoro* (I:20), *Evendimo* (I:322), *Everardo* (I:48), *Feanoro* (I:402), *fleto* (I:450), *Fornosto* (I:21), *Fredegaro* (I:66), *Frogmortono* (III:358), *Gandalfo* (I:30), *Gil-Galado* (I:78), *Glamdringo* (II:135), *Gondoro* (I:21), *Gorbago* (II:420), *Hamfasto* (I:39), *Isengardo* (I:527), *Isengrimo* (I:18), *Legolaso* (I:316), *miruvoro* (I:383), *Mordoro* (I:67), *Peregrino* (I:66), *periano* (III:167), *Sarumano* (I:73), *talano* (I:450), *Toboldo* (I:26), *Zirak-Zigilo* (I:373).

Sometimes Auld even modifies readily interpretable names in this manner, as such examples as *Bag-Endo* and *Bankso* demonstrate. A large number of names, however, require more than the simple suffixation of *-o* to Esperantize them; we will return to these later. On the other hand, a few names already conform to Esperanto orthography and morphology, so the Esperanto versions in (4) show no change. Note, however, that not all of these names are pronounced in Esperanto as they are in English.

(4) *Bilbo* (I:17), *Brego* (II:142), *Drogo* (I:39), *Frodo* (I:19), *Hugo* (I:59), *Milo* (I:59), *Odo* (I:50).

Affectionate diminutives of masculine names are formed in Esperanto by means of the suffix *-ĉjo*, and Auld occasionally makes use of this, sometimes even when the name in the original is not overtly marked as a diminutive, as the examples in (5) demonstrate.

(5) *Anĉjo* 'Andy' (I:455; but *Andio* II:262); *Dikuĉjo* 'Fatty' (I:99; cf. *Dikulo* in (1) above); *Froĉjo* 'Frodo' (I:49; cf. Frodo in (4) above); *Grimĉjo* 'Gríma' (III:336); *Grinĉjo* 'Pippin' (I:66); *Henĉjo* 'Harry' (I:206; *Henĉo* I:217 is a typographical error); *Nibĉjo* 'Nibs' (III:272); *Robĉjo* 'Cock-robin' (III:359; also *Robinĉjo* III:361); *Samĉjo* 'Sammy' (I:243); *Teĉjo* 'Ted' (I:93); *Toĉjo* 'Toby' (I:26); *Tomĉjo* 'Tom' (III:272); *Vilĉjo* 'Will' (I:212) and 'Bill' (I:222); but *Barlo* instead of *Barĉjo 'Barley' (I:216).

Auld's treatment of plural names is far from regular. In Esperanto, plural nouns are marked by the suffix *-oj*. Auld sometimes uses this suffix in place of Elvish or Old English plural markers, as in the examples in (6).

(6) *holbitloj* for *holbytlan* (II:195), *Malornoj* for *Mellyrn* (I:449), *Rohiroj* for *Rohirrim* (I:345).

In some instances, he adds this suffix to an already plural or collective form, as in the examples in (7).

(7) *edainoj* (II:348), *Eldaroj* (I:294), *Noldoroj* (II:244), *uruk-hajoj* (II:51).

In other instances, seen in (8), the plural suffix is added to a mangled element that is neither the singular nor the plural form of the name.

(8) *Forgoj* for *Forgoil* (II:169), *onodroj* for *onodrim* (II:49).[7]

In still other instances, such as those in (9), Auld adds a singular *-o* to a plural name with a plural or collective suffix.

(9) *Edoraso* (II:10), *Galadrimo* (I:448), *mearaso* (II:40).

Then there are some plurals, such as those in (10), which Auld treats in more than one of these ways.

(10) *smialoj* (I:24, II:72) and *Smialzoj* (III:388, in *Pli Bonaj Smialzoj* 'Better Smials'); *Valaro* (II:325) and *Valaroj* (III:314).

Feminine personal names generally receive a suffixed *-a* rather than *-o* in Auld's translation, as the examples in (11) demonstrate. The suffix *-a* is normally used to mark adjectives in Esperanto, but its use in feminine names is not unknown. Kalocsay and Waringhien (1980:65) interpret this as a use of a substantivally used adjective and thus as a grammatically legal construction.

(11) *Celebriana* (I:493), *Finduilasa* (III:306), *Galadriela* (I:464), *Melilota* (I:48), *Ungolianta* (II:406).

Of course, feminine names already ending in *-a* generally remain unchanged, as in (12).

(12) *Dora* (I:59), *Esmeralda* (I:50), *Lobelia* (I:47), *Varda* (I:497).

Esperanto also has a feminine counterpart of *-ĉjo*, namely *-njo*, used in forming affectionate diminutives and seen in (13).

(13) *Rozinjo* 'Rosie' (III:267).

Auld also replaces a number of names with hybrid forms, such as those in (14), combining modified and translated elements.

(14) *Bokelboro* 'Bucklebury' (I:36); *Brimonteto* 'Bree-hill' (I:201); *Dernkasko* 'Dernhelm' (III:90); *Etenerikejoj* 'Ettenmoors' (I:267); *Gajadoko* 'Meriadoc' (I:26); *Grizhejmo* 'Greyhame' (II:40, but in Esperanto = 'Greyhome'); *Hobiturbo* 'Hobbiton' (I:24); *Isenbuŝo* 'Isenmouthe' (III:10); *Malsekvango* 'Wetwang'

---

[7] The morpheme boundary in *onodrim* is before the *r*, not after it. The morphological structure of *Forgoil* is unknown.

(I:491); *Neĝburno* 'Snowbourn' (III:72); *Nikbrikuloj* 'Neekerbreekers' (I:246); *Ombrofakso* 'Shadowfax' (II:40); *Orvino* 'Goldwine' (III:326); *Pomodoro* 'Appledore' (I:211); *Pudipiedoj* 'Puddifoots' (I:130); *Sablomano* 'Sandyman' (I:40, but in Esperanto = 'Sand*hand*'); *Subharovo* 'Underharrow' (III:88); *Supraburno* 'Upbourn' (III:88); *Tajkampo* 'Tighfield' (II:262); *Ventfola* 'Windfola' (III:90).

Words and names that have been allowed to remain in their original forms are relatively rare in Auld's translation. Phrases and longer passages in Elvish and other non-English languages are generally unchanged, minor typographical errors notwithstanding.[8] Occasionally individual words also remain unaltered, such as the examples in (15).

(15) *ann-thennath* (I:259); *crebain* (I:376); *ghâsh* (I:430); *Ithil* (II:354); *ithildin* (I:418); *Lathspell* [sic, for *Láthspell*] (II:138); *lembas* (I:486, but *lembaso* I:510 and elsewhere); *simbelmynë* (III:67; *simbelmynd* II:131 is a typographical error); *tark/tarkil* (III:229 fn.); *Yrch* (I:453).

Auld hardly ever allows proper names to remain unaltered. The most notable exceptions are the monosyllabic names (mainly of hobbits) shown in (16).

(16) *Hal* (I:68), *Ham* (I:38), *Sam* (I:38), *Ted* (I:68), *Tom* (I:166).

In the case of *Grip, Fang,* and *Wolf*, the names of Farmer Maggot's dogs, Auld translates the names according to their meanings but keeps them monosyllabic by dropping the final *-o*, as we see in (17).

(17) *Ten, Dent, Lup* (I:130).

Sometimes, however, Auld does add the suffix *-o* to monosyllabic names, as in (18).

(18) *Bobo* (I:208), *Mato* (III:347), *Nobo* (I:208).

There are further examples of names that remain in their original forms, though we should expect them to have been modified. As the examples in (19) show,

---

8 See I:115, 313, 383, 394, 405-06, 449, 463, 496; II:52, 80, 144, 151, 401, 413; III:242, 294, 314, 319, 329, 332, 396.

these are almost exclusively either single instances of names that normally appear in modified form or else names that appear in verse.

(19) *Amon Hen* (II:17 only; cf. *Amono Hen* I:513); *Celos* (III:189, in verse); *Dagorlad* (I:320 only; cf. *Dagorlado* II:250); *Dior* (I:260 only; cf. *Dioro* I:320); *Dorthonion* (II:82, in verse); *Erui* (III:189, in verse); *Helm* (II:168, as exclamation; cf. *Helmo* passim); *Nan-tasarion* (II:82, in verse); *Ossir/ Ossiriand* (II:82, in verse); *Peregrin* (I:143 only; cf. *Peregrino* passim); *Tasarinan* (II:82, in verse; cf. *Tasarinano* III:333); *Taur-na-Neldor* (II:82, in verse).

3 Problem Spots

a) Treatment of non-Esperanto sounds and spellings

We have already seen how names have been modified to conform with Esperanto morphology by adding the proper suffixes. The problem of modifying names that contain non-Esperanto sounds and spellings is considerably more difficult and opens the door to many more inconsistencies.

In assimilating English names and names with English-style spellings, Auld vacillates between representing English sounds and representing English spellings, as the examples in (20) demonstrate.

(20) *Andio* 'Andy' (II:262), *Anĝelika* 'Angelica' (I:59), *Baginzo* 'Baggins' (I:32), *Bofino* 'Boffin' (I:66), *Bresgirdeloj* 'Bracegirdles' (I:46), *Brio* 'Bree' (I:21), *Brokhusoj* 'Brockhouses' (I:46), *Buĝfordo* 'Budgeford' (I:150), *Derndinglo* 'Derndingle' (II:94), *Dimrila* 'Dimrill' (adj., I:362), *Entmuto* 'Entmoot' (II:93), *Entvaŝo* 'Entwash' (I:491), *falohidoj* 'Fallowhides' (I:20), *Golumo* 'Gollum' (I:30), *Grimslado* 'Grimslade' (III:152), *Gruboj* 'Grubbs' (I:46), *harfutoj* 'Harfoots' (I:20), *hobito* 'hobbit' (I:17), *Holino* 'Hollin' (I:373), *Julo* 'Yule' (III:387), *Litho* 'Lithe' (III:387 fn.), *Mariŝo* 'Marish' (I:24), *Nibzo* 'Nibs' (III:367), *Nokso* 'Noakes' (I:39), *olifonto* 'oliphaunt' (II:306), *Raŝeo* 'Rushey' (I:36), *Raŭlo* 'Rowlie' (III:347), *reteo* 'Rethe' (III:293 fn.), *Ridermarko* 'Riddermarko' (I:345), *Rivendelo* 'Rivendell' (I:20), *Rorio* 'Rory' (I:50), *Roza* 'Rose' (III:390), *Rumblo* 'Rumble' (III:390), *Skario* 'Scary'

(III:386), *Stoko* 'Stock' (I:36), *sturoj* 'Stoors' (I:20), *Svertingoj* 'Swertings' (II:307), *Ŝarko* 'Sharkey' (III:363), *Ŝeloba* 'Shelob' (II:397), *Ŝirifo* 'Shirriff' (I:29), *Tindroko* 'Tindrock' (I:491), *Tjukboro* 'Tuckborough' (I:24), *Tjuko* 'Took' (I:18), *Vitvelo* 'Whitwell' (III:42).

In a number of the names in (20), such as *Baginzo* and *Bofino*, we find that double consonants have been simplified. This is usual in the creation of Esperanto words, and double consonants are generally only retained when simplification would cause confusion, as in *Finno* 'Finn' vis-à-vis *fino* 'end'.[9] Auld treats not only English names in this manner, but also names in the Elvish languages, as shown in (21). This is rather unfortunate, especially in instances in which the double consonant represents the final consonant of one element of a compound and the beginning consonant of another, as in *Leben-nin* and *Min-dol-luin*.

(21) *Eladano* (I:300), *Elesaro* (I:493), *Ereseo* (I:322), *Fen Holeno* (III:120), *Henet Anuno* (II:250), *Kormaleno* (III:287), *Lasemista* (II:100), *Lebenino* (I:390), *malorno* (I:449), *Min-Rimono* (III:12), *Mindoluino* (II:354), *Moranono* (II:250), *Pelenoro* (III:14), *Ramaso* (III:15), *Siranono* (I:396).

We have to assume that such assimilated forms are to be pronounced as in Esperanto, with the accent always on the penultimate syllable (Kalocsay and Waringhien 1980:40). The rules for accent in Elvish are quite different, and the placement of accent is frequently determined by whether or not a consonant is doubled or whether a vowel is short or long (Tolkien 1965:394). The latter distinction is also obscured by Auld, who in Esperantizing names deletes the acute accents and circumflexes that mark long vowels, as we find in the examples in (22).

(22) *Anariono* (I:320), *Andurilo* (I:365), *Daino* (I:302), *Deagolo* (I:79), *Deoro* (III:326), *Dino* (III:129), *Druadano* (III:126), *Dunadano* (I:305), *Eomero* (II:36), *Eomundo* (II:36), *eoredo* (II:39), *Felarofo* (II:132), *Floio* (I:423), *Fraro* (I:424), *Frealafo* (III:326), *Galmodo* (II:140), *Garulfo* (II:45), *Gloino* (I:301), *gorgunoj* (pl., III:129), *Hurino* (I:358), *Lonio* (I:424), *Lorieno* (I:300), *Lugburzo* (II:53), *Morgulo* (I:291), *Mumako* (II:325), *Nalio* (I:424), *Nazgulo* (II:54), *Numenoro* (I:260), *Nurneno*

---

9 Cf. Kalocsay and Waringhien (1980:27).

(II:293), *Oino* (I:302), *Olorino* (II:337), *Orod-na-Thon* (II:82, in verse), *palantiro* (II:240), *Rhuno* (I:327), *Ringlo* (III:45), *Rumilo* (I:450), *Smeagolo* (I:79), *Tinuviela* (I:257), *Turino* (I:358), *Uduno* (I:434), *Ugluko* (II:53), *Undomiela* (I:300).

Auld also modifies the spellings of names when they contain letters not found in Esperanto or letters that are used with phonetic values that differ from their values in Esperanto orthography. In some instances, Auld's substitutions are perfectly justifiable. The letter *y*, for example, is not found in the Esperanto alphabet, in which the letter *j* has the value of English *y*. Auld thus rightly substitutes *j* for *y* in the first four examples in (23). However, he inconsistently (and wrongly) substitutes *i* for *y* in *Kalacirio* (from *Calacirya*).

(23) *Envinjataro* (III:172), *Narja* (III:398), *Nenja* (I:480), *Vilja* (III:396); *Kalacirio* (I:497)

Auld also replaces the vocalic *y* found in Sindarin and Old English, as in (24). While this may agree with the Gondorian pronunciation of Sindarin *y* (Tolkien 1965:393), it is a rather unfortunate substitution.

(24) *Emin Muilo* (I:491), *Eovina* (II:141), *holbitloj* (II:195), *Roherino* (III:55), *Stibo* (III:55), *Trihirno* (II:156).

Conversely, some instances of *i* may properly be rendered in Esperanto by *j*: in the diphthongs *ai*, *ei*, etc., as well as initially in such Sindarin names as *Ioreth*. Auld makes this change in a number of names, shown in (25).

(25) *Ajgloso* (I:321), *Ejlenaĥo* (III:12), *Ered Nimrajso* (I:340), *Gvajhiro* (I:345), *hitlajno* (I:489), *Joreta* (III:168), *Morgajo* (III:220), *Rat Celedrajno* [*sic*, for *Rath Celerdain*] (III:41), *uruk-hajoj* (II:51).

However, he is not consistent in this regard, as the examples in (26) demonstrate. Note that the rules of Esperanto dictate that such combinations as *ai* and *ui* be pronounced as dissyllables rather than as diphthongs.

(26) *Anduino* (I:320), *Bruineno* (I:271), *Duinhiro* (III:45), *Duilino* (III:45), *edainoj* (II:348), *Emin Muilo* (I:491), *Eredo Litui* (II:293), *Fanuidolo* (I:373), *Finduilasa* (III:306), *Hirluino* (III:45), *Iorlaso* (III:42), *Mindoluino*

(II:354), *Miteitelo* (I:267), *Morgulduino* (II:371), *Naito* (I:456), *Orodruino* (I:90), *Tranduilo* (I:316).

Furthermore, in a couple of instances (27), he erroneously uses *j* when he should have retained the *i*.

(27) *Eregjono* (I:71, but *Eregiono* I:319), *Karnemirja* (II:100).

Finally, there are instances (28) in which Auld wrongly replaces *ai* with either *a* or *e*.

(28) *Eotano* (II:39); *Fornosto Ereno* (III:349), *Gilreno* (III:189), *Iarven Ben-Adar* (I:350).

Just as Esperanto *j* has the value of English *y*, the Esperanto letter *ŭ* has the value of English *w*. Consequently, Auld replaces most occurrences of the diphthong *au/aw* with *aŭ*, as we see in (29).

(29) *Amono Laŭ* (I:521), *Laŭrelindorinano* (II:80), *Maŭhuro* (II:64), *Raŭroso* (I:484), *Samato Naŭr* (III:278), *Saŭrono* (I:77), *Smaŭgo* (I:303), *Taŭremormalomo* [*sic*, for *Tauremornalómë*] (II:82).

However, he makes a few deviations from this practice, either retaining an original *au*, which is pronounced dissyllabically in Esperanto, or changing the w in *aw* to *v*, as shown in (30).

(30) *Tauremorno* (II:82), *Taur-na-Neldor* (II:82); *Aravo* (III:22).

The letter *ŭ* is generally only used for the diphthongal offglide, and the substitution of *v* for *w* is in fact normal in Esperanto, as in *Vaŝingtono* 'Washington'.[10] Thus, as we have already seen in the assimilations of such English names in (20) as *Vitvelo* 'Whitwell' (III:42), Auld uses *v* for *w*, even in Elvish and Anglo-Saxon names, such as those in (31).

(31) *Arvena* (I:300), *Deorvino* (III:147), *Dvalino* (I:302), *Dvimorbergo* (III:65), *Dvimordeno* (II:139), *Elvinga* (I:260), *Eovina* (II:141), *Folkvino* (III:326), *Freovino* [*sic*, for *Fréawine*] (III:326), *Gleovino* (III:325), *Gutvineo* (II:165),

---

10 This is not an absolute rule, however, as *ŭato* 'watt' demonstrates.

Gvajhiro (I:345), *Holdvino* (III:327), *Iarven Ben-Adar* (I:350), *Valdo* (III:326), *vargoj* 'wargs' (I:294), *Vidfaro* (III:135).

Certain consonantal spellings that are alien to Esperanto have been replaced by phonetic equivalents in normal Esperanto orthography. Thus *ph* is replaced by *f* (32) and *sh* by *ŝ* (33).

(32) *Efelo Duad* (II:293), *Ferianado* (III:94), *nifredilo* (I:460), *Orofino* (I:450).

(33) [In addition to English names in (20)] *Bunduŝaturo* (I:373), *Griŝnaĥo* (II:54), *Lugduŝo* (II:57), *Muzgaŝo* (III:229), *Ŝagrato* (II:420), *ŝarkû* (III:382 fn.).

Some consonant+*h* spellings, however, have been modified by means of eliminating the *h*. Auld replaces *gh* with *g*, *lh* with *l*, and *rh* with *r*, though he retains the *rh* spelling in his representation of *Rhûn* (34).

(34) *Gan-Buri-Gano* (III:129), *Amono Laŭ* (I:521), *Rosgobelo* (I:338); *Rhuno* (I:327).

The combination *ch* represents two different sounds in the names in *The Lord of the Rings*. It represents the affricate [tʃ] (as in *church*) in English names but the voiceless velar fricative [x] (as in *Bach*, *loch*) in names from other languages, such as Sindarin. The former is represented by the letter *ĉ* in Esperanto, as demonstrated by the examples in (35).

(35) *Ĉuboj* (I:46), *Fenmarĉo* (III:89), *Sanĉo* (I:62), *Telĉaro* (II:136).

Telĉaro is most likely an inaccurate rendering. Although the language of this name is uncertain, the *ch* of *Telchar* most probably should be represented by *ĥ*, which has the value [x], as in the examples in (36).

(36) *Arnaĥo* (III:153), *Ejlenaĥo* (III:12), *Ereĥo* (III:10), *Karaĥo Angren* (III:248), *Karĥosto* (III:221), *Losarnaĥo* (III:10), *Marĥo* (I:21), *Narĥosto* (III:221), *Toreĥo Ungol* (II:397).

There are inconsistencies here, as well, as the examples in (37) demonstrate. In the case of *Chetwood*, Auld had difficulty deciding whether to use *ĉ* or *ĥ*. Similarly,

Auld renders *Archet* either with *ĉ* or *k*. He also uses *k* in his representation of *Rammas Echor*, though *ĥ* would have represented the sound accurately.

(37) *Ĉetarbaro* (I:203), *Ĥetarbaro* (I:21); *Arĉeto* (III:347), *Arketo* (I:203); *Ramaso Ekor* (III:15).

The combination *kh* likewise represents two different sounds. It is the voiceless velar fricative [x] in Adûnaic, Black Speech, and Orkish, but an aspirated *k* in Khuzdul. Auld is apparently unaware of this, and he replaces *kh* with *ĥ* in both cases, as shown in (38). His rendering of *Khand*, which uses the combination *kĥ*, is bizarre as well as inconsistent.

(38) *Griŝnaĥo* (II:54), *Ĥazad ai-mênu* (II:166, 168), *Ĥazad-Dumo* (I:317), *Ĥeled-Zaramo* (I:374, but *Ĥeled-Zaram* II:182); *Kĥando* (III:149).

In Esperanto, the letter *c* always has the value [ts]. Consequently, Auld replaces *c* with *k* in those instances that he believes the pronunciation to be [k], as the examples in (39) demonstrate.

(39) *Ankalagono* (I:90), *Blanko* (I:21), *Folko* ([=Folco] I:66; [=Folca] III:326), *Folkvino* (III:326), *Gorbadoko* (I:39), *Inkanuso* (II:337), *Kalembel* (III:71), *Kalenardhono* (II:347), *Kalenhado* (III:12), *Karadraso* (I:373), *Karaĥo Angren* (III:248), *Karas Galadono* (I:464), *Karĥosto* (III:221), *Karn Dum* (I:195), *Karnemirja* (II:100), *Karoko* 'Carrock' (I:302), *Kormaleno* (III:287), *kram/kramo* (I:486), *Kuruniro* (II:104), *orkoj* (I:30), *Orkristo* (I:369), *Ortanko* (I:340), *Saradoko* (II:194), *Skato* 'Scatha' (III:328), *Telkontaro* (III:172).

In the transliteration of Elvish words, *c* always has the value [k]. Auld, however, appears to believe that *c* has the value [ts] before the front vowels *e* and *i*, as shown by the examples in (40).

(40) *Celebdilo* (I:373), *Celeborno* (I:464), *Celebranto* (I:448), *Celebriana* (I:493), *Celebrimboro* (I:319), *Cerino Amroto* (I:460), *Cirdano* (I:316), *Cirilo* (III:71), *Ciriono* (II:347), *Cirito Ungol* (II:250), *Kalaciriano* (I:310), *Kalacirio* (I:497), *Rat Celedrajno* [sic] (III:41).

At one occurrence of *Cirith Gorgor*, Auld correctly uses *k* rather than *c*. He also uses *k* in his Esperantization of the Rohirric Old English name *Ceorl*, which is incorrect, since the *c* in this name is to be pronounced as Esperanto *ĉ* (41).

(41) *Kirit Gorgoro* (I:491, but *Cirito Gorgor* II:293); *Keorlo* (II:157).

Finally, we come to the problem of *th*. This is generally used by Tolkien to represent the voiceless interdental fricative, as in English *thin*, a sound that does not occur in Esperanto. In most instances, such as those in (42), Auld replaces *th* with *t*, which represents a very different sound.

(42) *Amroto* (I:447), *Asfaloto* (I:284), *Atelaso* (I:265), *Berutiela* (I:410), *Bunduŝaturo* (I:373), *Eredo Litui* (II:293), *Fimbretila* (II:90), *Galatiliono* (III:320), *Gotmogo* (III:149), *Gutlafo* (III:145), *Gutvineo* (II:165), *Henet Anuno* (II:250), *hitlajno* (I:489), *Joreta* (III:168), *Kirit Gorgoro* (I:491), *lebetrono* (II:368), *Litlado* (II:293), *Lotlorieno* (I:437), *Lutiena* (I:259), *Malbeto* (III:59), *Meretrondo* (III:323), *Metedraso* (II:32), *Miteitelo* (I:267), *Mitlondo* (II:245), *Mitrandiro* (I:472), *mitrilo* (I:418), *Morgoto* (I:468), *Naito* (I:456), *Nargotrondo* (I:416), *Nimloto* (III:320), *Ortanko* (I:340; similarly *ortank* II:192), *Part Galeno* (I:520), *Pinato Gelin* (III:45), *Rat Dineno* (III:120), *Samato Naŭr* (III:278), *Skato* (III:328), *Tangorodrimo* (I:320), *Tarbado* (I:20), *Tarkuno* (II:337), *Tengelo* (II:37), *Teodeno* (II:37), *Teodredo* (II:138), *Tingolo* (I:259), *Torino* (I:30), *Torondoro* (III:287), *Traino* (I:254), *Tranduilo* (I:316), *Trihirno* 'Thrihyrne' (II:156; first element possibly translated: Esperanto *tri* 'three'), *Troro* (I:317).

However, in some instances, as in (43), Auld replaces *th* with *d*. Perhaps he does this believing that in these cases *th* is pronounced as a voiced interdental fricative (as in English *that*), which likewise does not occur in Esperanto. In the representation of Elvish, however, *th* is always voiceless, so Auld's *t/d* distinction is completely misleading. It is not even remotely logical, since we find him using *t* for *Amroth* and *Sammath* but *d* for *Esgaroth* and *Remmirath*.

(43) *Esgarodo* (I:49) [*Esgardodo* I:302 is presumably a typographical error], *Ferianado* (III:94), *Lodo* (I:100), *madomo* (I:23), *Neldoredo* (I:259), *Nimbredilo* (I:308), *Odo* 'Otho' (I:47; identical in form to *Odo* 'Odo' I:50), *Remirado* (I:116).

Even worse, we find several instances, seen in (44), in which Auld vacillates between *t* and *d* in the modification of a single name.

(44) *Aradorno* (I:292) vs. *Aratorno* (I:451)
[*Arahorno*, which only occurs at I:231, is probably a typographical error];
Argonado (I:323) vs. *Argonato* (I:513);
Denedoro (I:325) vs. *Denetoro* (I:530);
Doriado (I:320) vs. *Doriato* (II:405);
Elbereta (I:114) vs. *Elbereda* (I:314);
Efelo Duad (II:293) vs. *Efelo Duat* (II:373);
Giltonielo/Giltoniel' (I:113-14) vs. *Gildoniel'* (I:262);
Gorgorodo (I:322) vs. *Gorgoroto* (I:528);
Osgiliado (I:322) vs. *Osgiliato* (I:514).

In a few names, as in (45), Auld actually retains the original *th*. This leads to still more inconsistencies, as we find in the examples in (46).

(45) *Dorthonion* (II:82, in verse), *Nen Hithoelo* (I:484), *Orod-na-Thon* (II:82, in verse), *Ufthako* (II:427).

(46) *Etir Anduino* (I:527) vs. *Ethiro* (III:45);
itildin (I:402) vs. *ithildin* (I:418) and *Ithil* (II:354);
Mortondo (II:10) vs. *Morthondo* (III:10).

Auld generally uses *d* in place of *dh*, which in the representation of Sindarin represents the voiced interdental fricative (*th* in *that*), as shown in (47). An exception is his version of *Calenardhon*, which retains the spelling *dh*. It should be noted that Tolkien also occasionally used *d* in place of *dh*, as the forms *Galadrim* and *Caras Galadon* in earlier editions of *The Lord of the Rings* demonstrate.

(47) *Fanuidolo* (I:373), *Galadrimo* (I:448), *Karadraso* (I:373), *Karas Galadono* (I:464); *Kalenardhono* (II:347).

b) Treatment of original final vowel

Another way in which Auld's modification of names is inconsistent lies in his treatment of those names that end in vowels other than *o* or (for feminine or adjectival names) *a*. In a number of names, such as those in (48), Auld retains the original final vowel and places the appropriate grammatical suffix after it.

(48) *Dorio* (I:302), *Floio* (I:423), *Gimlio* (I:316), *Gutvineo* (II:165), *Kibil-Nalao* (I:374, but *Kibil-Nala* I:468), *Lonio* (I:424), *Nalio* (I:424), *Narvio* (I:402), *Norio* (I:302), *Orio* (I:302), *Oromeo* (III:138).

However, in others, such as those in (49), he deletes the final vowel before attaching the grammatical suffix.

(49) *Aldalomo* (II:82), *Ambarono* (II:82), *Arveduo* (I:21), *aseo aranion* (III:175), *Deorvino* (III:147), *Dunhero* (III:75), *Dvimordeno* (II:139), *Ereseo* (I:322), *Foldo* (III:89), *Folko* 'Folca' (III:326)[11], *Folkvino* (III:326), *Freo* (III:326), *Freovino* [sic] (III:326), *Gleovino* (III:325), *Grimo* (II:140), *Hamo* (II:134), *Herefaro* (III:153), *Holbitlo* (III:85), *Holdvino* (III:327), *Irensago* (III:77), *Kalacirio* (I:497), *Karnemirja* (II:100), *Leofo* (III:326), *Morio* (I:317), *Orofarna* (II:100), *Orvino* (III:326), *Skato* (III:328), *Snago* (II:60), *Stibo* (III:55), *Taŭremormalomo* [sic] (II:82), *Tauremorno* (II:82), *Trihirno* (II:156), *Valdo* (III:326), *Vidfaro* (III:135).

Auld's general tendencies, then, are to delete final *a* and *e* but to retain final *i*. He is not entirely consistent, however, as we see in *Kibil-Nalao* (*Kibil-nâla*), *Gutvineo* (*Guthwinë*), *Oromeo* (*Oromë*), and *Arveduo* (*Arvedui*).

In a couple of instances (50), Auld deletes more than just a final vowel before adding the noun suffix *-o*. In the case of *galeno* (from *galen-as* 'green-leaf'), he has in fact deleted an entire morpheme.

(50) *galeno* (I:27; but *galenaso* III:182), *Geronto* 'Gerontius' (II:73).

---

11 *Folko* represents 'Folco' at I:66.

c) Masculine/neuter names in -a, feminines in -o

We have seen how Auld's Esperantized versions of the names of male characters generally end in *-o* but those of female characters generally end in *-a*. However, since the suffix *-o* appears on common nouns and *-a* appears on adjectives, there are occasionally male characters whose names end in *-a* and female characters whose names end in *–o*.

Names ending in *-a* that are clearly adjectival rather than feminine occur in several instances, as shown in (51).

(51) The names of the hobbits' ponies: *Akrorela* 'Sharp-ears' (lit. 'sharp-eared'), *Saĝnaza* 'Wise-nose' (lit. 'wise-nosed'), *Flirtvosta* 'Swish-tail' (lit. 'swish-tailed'), *Fola* 'Bumpkin' (actually 'foolish, silly'), *Blankŝtrumpa* 'White-socks' (lit. 'white-stockinged'), *Grasul' Pendola* 'Fatty Lumpkin' (lit. 'pendulous fat one') (I:196);
The names of the Three Rings: *Narja* (III:398), *Nenja* (I:480), *Vilja* (III:396);
Adjectival nicknames of male hobbits: *Gaja* 'Merry' (I:60), *Ĝoja* 'Jolly' (I:60, III:272, 367; but *Ĝojo* III:373).

Auld also retains the original ending *-a* in *Ventfola* (see (14)), although the final *a* of Rohirric Old English *Windfola* is a masculine ending.

Conversely, some female characters have been given names ending in *-o*, as in (52), since their names are also common nouns. This is not always the case, however, as the example *Primola* demonstrates.

(52) *Kalendulo* 'Marigold' (III:267), *Orbero* 'Goldberry' (I:167); but *Primola* (I:39; *primolo* 'primula').

In a couple of instances (53), Auld uses the different suffixes to distinguish between a female character and a flower or river.

(53) *elanoro* [flower] vs. *Elanora* [Sam's daughter] (III:393);
Nimrodelo [river] (I:445) vs. *Nimrodela* [elf-woman] (I:446).

A few names, however, appear with both suffixes without any justification. These are shown in (54).

(54) *Elbereta* (I:114), but *Elbereto* (I:114, in verse);
Giltoniela (I:509), but *Giltonielo* (I:113, in verse);
Limlumo 'Limlight' (I:501), but *Limluma* (II:10).

d) Treatment of names consisting of more than one word

Names consisting of more than one word, especially Sindarin place-names, are not infrequent in *The Lord of the Rings*. These usually have the structure *noun + (genitive) noun* or *noun + adjective*, and consequently they pose something of a problem for Auld's practice of tacking a noun suffix onto the end of a name. Should the suffix be added to the first word, the second word, both words, or neither? Auld does all of these things, as examples (55)–(58) clearly show.

(55) *-o* on first word: *Amono Hen* (I:513), *Amono Laŭ* (I:521), *aseo aranion* (III:175), *Cirito Ungol* (II:250), *Efelo Duad* (II:293), *Eredo Litui* (II:293), *Imlado Morgul* (II:367), *Karaho Angren* (III:248), *Minaso Anor* (I:322), *Minaso Itil* (I:322), *Minaso Morgul* (I:323), *Pinato Gelin* (III:45), *Samato Naŭr* (III:278), *Toreho Ungol* (II:397).

(56) *-o* on second word: *Dol Barano* (II:234), *Dol Gulduro* (I:330), *Etir Anduino* (I:527), *Fen Holeno* (III:120), *Karas Galadono* (I:464), *Nan Kuruniro* (II:104), *Nen Hithoelo* (I:484), *Rat Celedrajno [sic]* (III:41), *Rat Dineno* (III:120), *Tol Brandiro* (I:491).

(57) *-o* on both words: *Cerino Amroto* (I:460), *Fornosto Ereno* (III:349), *Imloto Meluio* (III:176).

(58) *-o* not added: *Iarven Ben-Adar* (I:350), *Karn Dum* (I:195).

It is difficult, if not impossible, to find any rhyme or reason in Auld's placement of the singular noun suffix in these names. Many singular nouns have been allowed to stand without the suffixed *-o*, whereas Auld has attached it to such plural nouns as *erain* 'kings', *pinnath* 'ridges', and *sammath* 'chambers', as well as to such adjectives as *baran* 'golden brown', *dínen* 'silent', and *hollen* 'closed'. It is quite clear that Auld understands very little about the Elvish languages.

There are also inconsistencies with respect to the treatment of individual names. In the case of a few two-word names in which only one of the words has been suffixed, the unsuffixed word appears with the suffix when on its own, as in (59).

(59) *Amono Din* (III:12) vs. *Dino* (III:129);
Etir Anduino (I:527) vs. *Ethiro* (III:45);
Kairo Andros (III:10) vs. *Androso* (III:114).

Even worse, there are a number of names in which the suffixation varies from occurrence to occurrence, as we see in (60).

(60) *Amono Sulo* (I:249) vs. *Amono Sul* (II:245);
Emin Arneno (III:15) vs. *Emino Arnen* (III:10);
Emin Muilo (I:491) vs. *Emino Muil* (III:204);
Ered Nimrajso (I:340) vs. *Eredo Nimrajs* (II:346);
Henet Anuno (II:250) vs. *Heneto Anun* (III:204);
Kirit Gorgoro (I:491) vs. *Cirito Gorgor* (II:293);
Minaso Tirit (I:323) vs. *Minas Tirito* (I:471);
Part Galeno (I:520, II:12) vs. *Parton Galenon* (II:19, in accusative case);
Sarn Gebiro (I:484) vs. *Sarno Gebir* (I:512).

4 Inexplicable Inconsistencies

The vast majority of the inconsistencies that we have examined so far have their roots in the difficulties inherent in assimilating names into Esperanto. Now we come to inconsistencies that cannot be explained away in such a manner.

a) Sounds and letters arbitrarily changed

We have seen a considerable number of names that have been changed because they contained sounds or spellings that are alien to Esperanto. There are also several names, listed in (61), in which Auld has altered sounds and spellings that would be perfectly acceptable in Esperanto.

(61) *Anfalas* > *Enfalaso* (III:45);
Angrenost > *Argenosto* (II:87);
Arvernien > *Avernino* (I:308);
Bombadil > *Bombadiljo* (I:166 et seq.);
Durthang > *Dartango* (III:260, 265);
Eärendil > *Erendilo* (I:260, I:308, II:390);
Gram > *Gremo* (III:326);
Halbarad > *Halberado* (III:50 et seq.);
Menelvagor > *Menelvagro* (I:116);
Rath Celerdain > *Rat Celedrajno* (III:41);
Silvertine > *Sivertino* (I:373, II:123) [this should have been translated rather than adapted].

A few of these may have been altered because a straight adaptation would have yielded an Esperanto word with a different meaning, thus *Gramo 'gram (unit of mass)' and *Halbarado 'the action of blocking up a hall'. This is almost certainly the rationale behind rendering Bombadil as Bombadiljo, since *Bombadilo would be interpreted by an Esperanto reader as 'an implement for continual bombing'. However, most of these modifications, such as *Argenosto* and *Avernino*, cannot be justified in any way.

b) Translation vs. adaptation

There are also several names, shown in (62), which have a translated form at one occurrence but an assimilated form at another.

(62) Bagshot Row: *Baĝŝuta Vico* (I:38), *Baĝŝota Vico* (I:477);
Haysend: *Fojnofino* (I:159), *Hejsendo* (I:36);
Hornburg: *Kornburgo* (II:158), *Hornburgo* (III:195);
Mark: *Limregno* (III:73), *Marko* (II:118);
Sackville-Bagginses: *Retikul-Baginzoj* (I:37), *Sakvil-Baginzoj* (I:360);
Samwise: *Samsaĝo* (I:32; usual), *Samvajso* (II:326 only);
Whitfoot: *Blankpiedo* (III:360), *Vitfuto* (I:212).

c) Sheer inconsistencies in chosen forms

Far more frequent, however, are the names that have simply been translated differently at various occurrences, as shown in (63).

(63) Barrow-downs: *Dolmenejoj* (I:180), *Dolmenejo* (I:185);
Bay of Belfalas: *Golfo de Belfalaso* (I:448), *golfo Belfalaso* (I:501);
Black Gate: *Nigra Pordo* (III:7), *Nigra Pordego* (III:205);
Brandywine Bridge: *Ponto Brandovino* (I:22), *Brandovina Ponto* (I:36);
city of the Galad(h)rim: *urbo Galadrimo* (I:460), *urbo de Galadrimo* (I:460);
Cracks of Doom: *Fendoj de Sorto* (I:531), *Fendajo de l'Destino* (II:351), *Fendajo de Sorto* (II:416), *Fendajoj de l'Destino* (III:275), *Fendajo de Destino* (III:284);
Dark Land: *Malluma Lando* (II:259), *Malhela Lando* (II:283);
Dark Lord: *Malhela Mastro* (I:77), *Malluma Mastro* (I:199);
Dark Tower: *Malhela Turo* (I:67), *Malluma Turo* (I:77), *Malhela Turego* (II:115);
Dark Years: *Malhelaj Jaroj* (III:16), *Mallumaj Jaroj* (III:60);
Deeping-coomb: *Profunda Kavajo* (II:159), *Profundaja Kavajo* (II:175);
dwarves: *gnomoj* (I:42), *nanoj* (I:391);
Floating Log: *Flosa Arbotrunko* (III:358), *Flosanta Arbotrunko* (III:359);
Ford of Bruinen: *transpasejo Bruineno* (I:252), *Transpasejo de Bruineno* (I:271);
Fords of Isen: *Travadejoj de Iseno* (II:10), *Trapasejoj de Iseno* (II:243);
Gaffer: *Avulo* (I:38), *Laborestro* (I:60), *oldulo* (I:109);
Gates of Argonath: *Pordoj de Argonato* (I:513), *Pordego de Argonato* (I:516);
goblins: *goblinaj* (adj., I:45), *koboldoj* (I:153), *goblenaj* (adj., II:14);
Golden Hall: *Ora Palaco* (II:146), *Ora Halo* (II:152);
Great River: *Riverego* (I:20), *Granda Rivero* (I:79);
Great Smials: *Grandaj Smialoj* (I:25), *Granda Smialo* (III:370);
Hornblower: *Kornblovulo* (I:26), *Kornblovo* (I:46);
Master Elrond: *Estro Elrondo* (I:304), *Mastro Elrondo* (I:323);
Master of the Hall: *mastro de l'Halo* (I:139), *Estro de la Halo* (I:149);
Misty Mountains: *Nebulecaj Montoj* (I:19), *Nebulecaj Montaroj* (I:223), *Nebuletaj Montoj* (I:296), *Nebuleca Montaro* (I:373);
Mountain of Fire: *Monto de Fajro* (I:319), *Fajromonto* (III:220);
Mountains of Shadow: *Monto de Ombroj* (I:322), *Montoj de Ombroj* (I:331), *Montoj de l'Ombro* (I:380), *Ombraj Montoj* (II:250), *Montoj de Ombro* (II:414);

Old Forest: *Malnova Arbaro* (I:36), *Malnova Arbarego* (I:39), *Maljuna Arbaro* (II:81);
Old Took: *Maljuna Tjuko* (I:38), *Olda Tjuko* (II:73);
Old Winyards: *Malnova Vinberejo* (I:60), *Malnovaj Vinberujoj* (I:99);
Precious: *trezorego* (I:30), *trezoro* (II:265);
Sarn Ford: *Transpasejo Sarno* (I:36), *trapasejo Sarno* (I:232), *Sarna Transpasejo* (III:357);
Sting: *Piko* (I:33), *Pikilo* (II:266);
Three-Farthing Stone: *Trikvarona Mejloŝtono* (III:361),*Tri-kvarona Ŝtono* (III:389);
Tower of Guard: *Turego Garda* (II:12), *Garda Tur'* (II:17, in verse);
Underhill: *Submonto* (I:92), *Submonteto* (I:202);
Westmarch: *Okcidentlimo* (I:17), *Okcidentejo* (I:22);
White Downs: *Blankaj Suprejoj* (I:24), *Blankaj Supraπoj* (I:29);
White Mountains: *Blankaj Montoj* (II:10), *Blanka Montaro* (II:23);
Wilderland: *Sovaĝujo* (I:331), *Sovaĝlando* (II:86);
Wood-elves: *arbarelfoj* (I:86), *arbaraj elfoj* (I:86).

In several of these examples, such as the translations of Dark Land, Wilderland, and Wood-elves, the differences are not semantically significant. In other instances, the semantic differences are minor, stemming from such things as the presence or absence of the augmentative element *-eg-* (as in the translations of Black Gate and Precious) or the presence or absence of the plural suffix (as in the translations of Barrow-downs or Great Smials). There are, however, instances in which at least one of the translations is demonstrably incorrect, such as *Ponto Brandovino*, which implies 'Bridge named Brandywine' rather than 'Bridge over the River Brandywine'; *Profunda Kavaĵo* 'Deep Hollow' for Deeping-coomb; and *Trikvarona Mejloŝtono* 'Three-Farthing Milestone' for the Three-Farthing Stone.

There are also a number of names that have been phonologically and morphologically modified in different ways, as shown in (64).

(64) Annúminas: *Annuminaso* (I:322, II:245), *Anuminaso* (III:321);
    Barad-dûr: *Baraduro* (I:391; usual), *Barad-Duro* (I:528 only);
    Bolger: *Bolĝero* (I:66; usual), *Bolgero* (I:153 only, probably a typo);

Dúnedain: *dunedanoj* (I:21 only), *Dunadanoj* (I:325; usual);
Dunharrow: *Dunharo* (II:145; usual), *Dunharovo* (III:77 only);
Emyn Muil: *Emin Muilo* (I:491, 512; usual), *Amin Muilo* (I:512 only, probably a typo);
Ernil i Pheriannath: *Ernil i Pheriannath* (III:41), *Ernilo i Ferianado* (III:94);
Halifirien: *Halifirieno* (III:12), *Halifireno* (III:90; cf. *Firenfeldo* III:77, *Firenarbaro* III:89);
Harrowdale: *Harvalo* (III:62), *Harovovalo* (III:72);
Ithilien: *Itilieno* (I:323 only), *Itilio* (II:10; usual);
Lune: *Ljuno* (I:21; usual), *Ljimo* (I:21; probably due to unclear handwriting in Auld's manuscript);
Norbury: *Norbrio* (I:28), *Norburio* (III:349).

Finally, perhaps the most frightening example of inconsistency in Auld's translation is his rendering of the place-name *Dale*, which appears in two different translated forms and two different adapted forms (65), all within the course of one volume.

(65) *Dalo* (I:30), *Valejo* (I:45), *Delo* (I:86), *Valo* (I:422).

5 Differences between the Esperanto Translations

Gledhill's translation of *The Hobbit*, which makes use of Auld's translations of the poems and which was published by the same firm as *La Mastro de l' Ringoj* naturally makes use of nomenclature that for the most part agrees with that of Auld's earlier publication. It improves upon Auld's work, however, by treating the names much more consistently. In *La hobito*, the word *gnomo* is always used for 'dwarf' (H:5), whereas Auld vacillates between *gnomo* and *nano* in *La Mastro de l' Ringoj* ((63) above). Gledhill always uses *Dalo* for 'Dale' (e.g. H:20), as opposed to Auld's *Dalo, Delo, Valo, Valejo* ((65) above). Furthermore, Gledhill always renders *th* as *t*, as shown in (66), rather than vacillating between *t*, *th*, and *d*.

(66) *Torino* (H:15), *Troro* (H:20), *Traino* (H:22), *Esgaroto* (H:162), *Bladortino* (H:166), *mitrilo* (H:173).

This leads to the one significant difference in nomenclature between *La hobito* and *La Mastro de l' Ringoj*: Esgaroth is rendered as *Esgaroto* in the former but as *Esgarodo* in the latter (see (43) above).

This is not to say that Gledhill's translation is entirely free of inconsistencies. There are, in fact, a few internal inconsistencies in the treatment of names, shown in (67), but these are relatively minor.

(67) Bag-End, Underhill: *Bag-Endo en Submonteto* (H:17), *Bag-Endo Sub la Monteto* (H:162);
Edge of the Wild: *Limo de Sovaĝujo* (H:46), *rando de Sovaĝujo* (H:75);
Side-door: *Flanka Pordo* (H:21), *Flankpordo* (H:25).

Koboldurb' 'Goblin-town' (H:48) might also be mentioned, since *gobleno* is used as the translation of 'goblin', but *koboldoj* is in fact used elsewhere in the book to translate 'hobgoblins' (H:102); cf. (63) above.

Like Auld (see (61) above), Gledhill makes a few arbitrary changes to some of the names, as shown in (68).

(68) *Arkenstone > Arkeŝtono* (H:167);
Dorwinion > Dorvinio (H:130);
Golfimbul > Golfumbulo (H:18);
Mount Gram > Monto Gramao (H:18).

The replacement of *stone* by its Esperanto equivalent *ŝtono* is perfectly reasonable, but I can see no reason why Gledhill used *Arkeŝtono* rather than **Arkenŝtono*. Similarly, why did he use *Dorvinio* rather than **Dorviniono* and *Golfumbulo* rather than **Golfimbulo*? The change of Gram to *Gramao* may have had the same motivation as Auld's rendering of Gram (King of Rohan) as *Gremo* (see (61) above), but the final *–ao* looks strange in any case.

Harlow's (1991) two-page excerpt from 'Inside Information', which also includes a brief synopsis of the story up to that point, naturally differs significantly from the later version by Gledhill and Auld. In both versions, readily interpretable names of peoples and places are translated into Esperanto. Some of these are identical in the two translations, such as *elfoj* 'elves', *goblenoj* 'goblins', *Laganoj* 'Lake-men', and *Soleca Monto* 'Lonely Mountain'. Other names differ, such as that of the Misty Mountains, which Gledhill calls *Nebulecaj Montoj* (H:38), but Harlow (1991:11) calls *Nebulmontaro*. Harlow (1991:12) also translates Bag-End as *Sakfundo*, whereas Auld and Gledhill use the Esperantized English *Bag-Endo*. The most curious place-name in Harlow's text is *Val* 'Dale'; he has translated the name into a form that would be understood by Esperanto speakers but which is not really an Esperanto form (*valo* = valley, dale).

Returning to the names of peoples, Harlow renders 'trolls' as *koboldoj*, whereas Auld and Gledhill use *troloj*, with *koboldoj* referring to (hob)goblins in their translations. Rather than using *gnomoj* or *nanoj*, Harlow calls his dwarves *dvarvoj*, a coinage that sticks closer to the English source.[12] Also closer to the original is Harlow's *hobbito*, as opposed to Auld and Gledhill's *hobito*. Harlow's Esperantization of 'orcs' as *aŭrkoj*, however, is an unwarranted and unfortunate modification.

The most striking difference between Harlow's translation on one hand and Auld and Gledhill's on the other is in the treatment of the proper names of individuals. Although he renders the place-name Esgaroth as *Esgaroto*, just as Gledhill does, Harlow leaves the names of characters for the most part unaltered: *Bilbo Baggins, Gandalf, Gollum, Girion*. No doubled consonants have been simplified, no *o*'s have been added. In changing the dragon's name to *Smaŭg*, Harlow is in fact preserving its form, since the rules of Esperanto pronunciation would require the original *Smaug* to be pronounced as a two-syllable word.

6 Conclusion

One question that should be addressed is whether or not non-Esperanto names should be modified to make them conform with the rules of Esperanto spelling and grammar in the first place. The usual practice in Esperanto is to use assimilated forms for the first names of persons, the most famous personal names from antiquity, names of continents, countries, and major cities and geographical features, whereas personal surnames and the names of lesser-known cities,

---

12 This could perhaps be likened to Tolkien's use of *dwarves* rather than *dwarfs* to "remove them a little, perhaps, from the sillier tales of these latter days" (Tolkien 1965:415).

towns, and geographical features tend to be rendered in Esperanto either in their original spelling or rendered phonetically in Esperanto orthography. It should be emphasized, however, that these are general tendencies and not rules.[13]

This leaves a lot of room for variation. There is in fact a gradient between unassimilated names and fully Esperantized forms, and Esperanto writers do not always agree on how to modify names. For example, in the *Fundamenta Krestomatio*, which is regarded as a model of good Esperanto style, we can find such assimilated forms as *Zeŭso* and *Kristoforo Kolumbo* beside such unassimilated names as *Allah* and *John Wilkins* (Zamenhof 1921:441, 98, 30, 258). Zamenhof (1921:vii) also notes that within the chrestomathy the name of Jesus is rendered variously as *Jesuo* and *Jezo* and that of Canada as *Kanadujo* and *Kanado*. It is therefore not surprising that there is some degree of inconsistency in how Auld modifies the names in *The Lord of the Rings*.

Be that as it may, it is still distressing to see just how inconsistent Auld's treatment of the names really is. Whereas arguments may be made for and against the rendering of *Elbereth* as *Elbereta*, for example, the fact that this name appears in the translation variously as *Elbereta*, *Elbereda*, and *Elbereto* is simply inexcusable. It is truly a pity that the first translation of *The Lord of the Rings* into an artificial language was not done with the care and attention to detail that such a project requires and deserves.

The strategies used by Gledhill in translating the names in *La hobito* do not differ significantly from those used by Auld in *La Mastro de l' Ringoj*, though Gledhill uses them in a more consistent manner. In this respect, Gledhill and Auld's translation of *The Hobbit* is better than Auld's version of *The Lord of the Rings*.[14] It is a shame, though, that Don Harlow did not translate more than a couple of pages of *The Hobbit*. I cannot say whether it would have been a better translation than Gledhill and Auld's, but it certainly would have been different.

---

13 Cf. Kalocsay and Waringhien (1980:63–67).
14 It should be noted, however, that *La hobito* contains deficiencies in other areas, particularly in the inept handling of the prefatory note and the addition of an absurd appendix of supposed etymologies of names. For a more detailed description, see Smith 2001.

Acknowledgement

I would like to thank Patrick Wynne, whose close reading of the Esperanto translations provided me with some interesting examples that I might otherwise have missed.

About the author

Arden R. Smith received a Ph.D. in Germanic Linguistics from the University of California, Berkeley, in 1997. He has published numerous articles in the field of Tolkien studies, especially concerning Tolkien's invented writing systems and the translation of Tolkien's works. His occasional column on the latter, 'Transitions in Translations', has appeared in the journal Vinyar Tengwar since 1989. He has also edited or co-edited a number of previously unpublished linguistic papers by Tolkien, including the corpus of material on the Alphabet of Rúmil, published in the journal Parma Eldalamberon in 2001.

References

AULD, William (trans.), *La Kunularo de l' Ringo*, (by J.R.R. Tolkien. Original title: *The Fellowship of the Ring*, 1954, second edition 1965), Jekaterinburg: Sezonoj, 1995.

(trans.), *La du turegoj*, (by J.R.R. Tolkien. Original title: *The Two Towers*, 1954, second edition 1965), Jekaterinburg: Sezonoj, 1996.

(trans.), *La reveno de la Reĝo*, (by J.R.R. Tolkien. Original title: *The Return of the King*, 1955, second edition 1965), Jekaterinburg: Sezonoj, 1997.

BENCZIK, Vilmos (ed.), *Lingva arto: Jubilea libro omaĝe al William Auld kaj Marjorie Boulton*, Rotterdam: Universala Esperanto-Asocio, 1999.

CIMPA, Christian, 'Bibliografio de William Auld', In: V. Benczik (ed.), *Lingva arto: Jubilea libro omaĝe al William Auld kaj Marjorie Boulton*, Rotterdam: Universala Esperanto-Asocio, 1999, 204–09.

GLEDHILL, Christopher, and William Auld (trans.), *La hobito, aŭ tien kaj reen*, (by J.R.R. Tolkien. Original title: *The Hobbit; or, There and Back Again*, 1937, third edition 1966), Jekaterinburg: Sezonoj, 2000.

HARLOW, Don (trans.), *La Hobbito: El Ĉapitro XII*, (by J.R.R. Tolkien. Original title: *The Hobbit; or, There and Back Again*, 1937, third edition 1966; excerpt from chapter XII), In: *ELNA Literatura Suplemento*, (1991), 11–12.

KALOCSAY, K., and G. Waringhien, *Plena analiza gramatiko de Esperanto*, (fourth edition, first edition 1935), Rotterdam: Universala Esperanto-Asocio, 1980.

KORĴENKOV, Aleksander, 1999, 'Unu ringo ilin regas', In: V. Benczik (ed.), *Lingva arto: Jubilea libro omaĝe al William Auld kaj Marjorie Boulton*, Rotterdam: Universala Esperanto-Asocio, 1999, 92–100.

NAGEL, Rainer, 'Normenvorgabe in der literarischen Übersetzung: Illustriert an den Eigennamen in J.R.R. Tolkiens *The Lord of the Rings*', In: *Zeitschrift für Anglistik und Amerikanistik* 43, (1995), 1–10.

SMITH, Arden R., 'Feature Book Review: J.R.R. Tolkien, *La hobito, aŭ tien kaj reen*', In: *Mythprint* 232, (July 2001) 4–6.

TOLKIEN, J.R.R., *The Return of the King*, (second edition, first edition 1955), Boston: Houghton Mifflin, 1965.

'Guide to the Names in *The Lord of the Rings*', In: Jared Lobdell (ed.), *A Tolkien Compass*, La Salle, Illinois: Open Court, 1975, 153–201.

ZAMENHOF, L.L. (ed.), *Fundamenta Krestomatio de la Lingvo Esperanto*, (eighth edition, first edition 1903), Paris: Esperantista Centra Librejo, 1921.

Mark T. Hooker

Nine Russian Translations of *The Lord of the Rings*

Abstract

Tolkien was banned in the Soviet Union, but that did not stop Russian translations of his works from circulating the illicit underground Russian press known as *samizdat*. The result of Tolkien's years of exile in samizdat, and the collapse of the state-controlled publishing industry when the Soviet Union disintegrated is that there is not just one published Russian translation of *The Lord of the Rings* as is common in other countries. There are nine contemporary published translations competing with each other for the reader's attention. Each translator has a slightly different approach to the text. Each translation has a slightly different interpretation of Tolkien. Each translator has a different story to tell. The goal of this paper is to point out the differences.

1 Introduction

In a typescript underground there lived a Hobbit. Not in a spell-checked, crisp, laser-printed typescript fresh from the computer, but in a dog-eared, crumpled, fifth-carbon-copy typescript full of spelling mistakes, typed by hand on the back of some document that was no longer needed. It was a *samizdat* typescript, and that meant illicit, underground publishing in the Soviet Union.

After the publication of J.R.R. Tolkien's *The Lord of the Rings* (1954-55), translations followed quickly in Holland (1956-57) and Sweden (1959-61), where translated literature is widely accepted. The Polish translation (1961-63) was right on the heels of the Swedish one and ahead of the Danish (1968-70), German (1969-70), and French (1972-73) translations, but the publication of a state-sanctioned Russian translation was a long time in coming in the totalitarian Soviet Union.

The publication of the Russian translation of *The Lord of the Rings* (*LotR*) was essentially banned by the state-controlled publishing industry in the USSR until 1982, when an abridged edition of Volume I of the trilogy – the one that is the least sensitive ideologically – was finally published. The unabridged edition of Volume I by the same officially sanctioned translators did not come out for another six years. After it was published in 1988, it was followed by the translations of Volumes II and III at two-year intervals in 1990 and 1992 in the wake of the Soviet collapse.

Samizdat, however, was another story. Samizdat was the opposite of the centralized Soviet-controlled publishing system. It was not a system at all, but rather a number of isolated groups of individuals who shared works of literature that were otherwise not available. The result of the isolation of the various groups was that a number of different translations of Tolkien's works began to circulate. Most often the translations were done by translators, whose imagination was captured by Tolkien's vision and who wished to share it with friends and family. They were neither paid nor encouraged to do so. In fact, they placed themselves at risk by producing the translations.

In the mid-1960s, the last years of the 'thaw' in Soviet literature that resulted from Khrushchev's efforts at de-Stalinization, Zinaida Anatol'evna Bobyr' produced a samizdat condensation of *LotR*. Bobyr' was one of the best among the translators who helped popularize translated science fiction in the 1950s. Bobyr's list of credits includes Brian Aldiss, Isaac Asimov, John Gordon, Edmond Hamilton, Clifford Simak and Stanislaw Lem, whom she translated from Polish.

The version of her samizdat condensation of *LotR* that survived into print in the 'publishing boom' that followed the collapse of Communism in the early 1990s is only one third as long as the original, and contains a number of embellishments to the story line. In her version, for example, in addition to the Ring of Power there is also a Silver Crown of the Lords of Westernesse, which is one of the greatest treasures brought from over the sea. "He who dares to place it upon his brow will either receive omniscience and the greatest of wisdom, or [...] will be turned to ashes on the spot, if he has not sufficiently prepared for it." (Bobyr' p. 67) If Aragorn is capable of wearing the Silver Crown, he will prove himself worthy of marriage to Arwen and of becoming Elrond's successor. The plot thickens, because the Silver Crown is in Osgiliath, which is in the hands of the Enemy. All is not lost, however, because Sauron knows that he dare not touch the Silver Crown without the Ring. In the end, Aragorn claims the Silver Crown for his own, in a happily-ever-after fairy-tale ending (Bobyr' p. 473).

Bobyr's condensation is almost universally dismissed as a hack job by the present generation of Russian Tolkienists, who have access to a number of full translations and even to the English original. In the context in which it first appeared, however, it was a daring effort at making Tolkien available – albeit in condensed form – to the Russian reading public, despite the unreceptive political climate of the Soviet, state-controlled publishing industry.

In about 1975, Aleksandr A. Gruzberg produced a complete samizdat translation. Gruzberg, a linguist by profession, was secretly also a very active samizdat science fiction translator, working under the pen-name of D. Arsen'ev. His list of credits includes Poul Anderson, Isaac Asimov, Edgar Rice Burroughs, A. Norton and Perry Rhodan. Gruzberg discovered Tolkien in the Library of Foreign Literature in Moscow. He ordered a microfilm copy of the Trilogy from the library. This service was very inexpensive, especially when compared to buying real English-language books, which were hard to find in any event. The first version of his translation was written out entirely by hand. Typewriters were controlled items and computers were undreamed of at that time. It took him about a year to complete.

His translation of *LotR* circulated in the same way that his other samizdat science fiction translations did. The manuscripts were typed in six copies – copying machines were also controlled items – and sent off to Leningrad (now Saint Petersburg). From there, they circulated throughout the country.

Participation in the illicit publishing industry was not without its dangers. Gruzberg himself had a close call with the authorities because of his samizdat activities.

> You could be fired and prosecuted for that kind of thing. I was lucky. I had a close call once, when they found one of my translations at the home of an acquaintance of mine, whom they were accusing of distributing samizdat. They came out to see me, but only warned me that I should not do things like this any more. That was in 1985, I think, and for a long time after that incident, I stopped doing translations.

Reading a samizdat typescript of *LotR* had a special feeling to it. It was something to read alone, where no one else could see you reading it. While reading it – to a certain extent – you literally shared the dangers of the fellowship. The mere possession of this book was a criminal offense, though hardly anyone was prosecuted for this alone. The ideas contained in the book made a special impression on the reader, because the reader was taking a risk to learn what they were. If they were not special, anyone could read it. Evgeniya Smagina – one of the first to read Bobyr's samizdat text – said:

> reading uncensored, free speech gave you a feeling of freedom, a breath of fresh air (which made up for the literary imperfections of many of these texts). Besides that, there was a certain pride in yourself, a sense of your own courage, a euphoria from having performed a free, unsanctioned act, which must be hard to comprehend for a person who has lived their whole life under conditions of freedom of speech and the press.

The samizdat copy of a book was only on loan to you for three to four days and people stayed up all night and ignored their jobs and classes to read it. One informant memorized the text of *LotR* and became the book, bringing life to the fiction that was Ray Bradbury's *Fahrenheit 451*.

2 The First Translation Boom

In 1982, an abridged translation of Volume I of the Trilogy was officially published by the Children's Literature [Детская литература] Publishing House in Moscow. This translation was done by Vladimir Sergeevich Murav'ev and Andrej Andreevich Kistyakovskij (M&K), who had first read Tolkien in the early 1970s and were enthralled by him. They wanted to use Tolkien's trilogy as a "rather long, militant manifesto" for "the revolt of the prisoners of the GULAG," said C.S. Lewis scholar, and friend of the translators, Professor N.L. Trauberg.

The abridged translation was an immediate best seller. The initial print run of 100,000 copies sold out, and in 1983 Children's Literature Publishing House took the unusual step for a planned economy publishing house of printing two more runs totaling 300,000 copies. These extra copies, too, rapidly sold out and before long the book was not even available in libraries, as the copies were stolen from the shelves.

The publication of the abridged M&K translation of Volume I came at a politically inopportune time, at the height of the Cold War. On 8 June 1982, Ronald Reagan made his famous 'Evil Empire' speech in which some Tolkien scholars – both East and West – see clear allusions to Gandalf's speeches at the Council of Elrond in Chapter 2 of Book II and at the council in Aragorn's tents in Chapter 9 of Book V. In his article[1] 'Eurasian Tendencies in Domestic Fantasy Literature,' Anatolij Moshnitskij directly credits Reagan's 'quote' from Tolkien in the 'Evil Empire' speech for stopping the publication of the next two volumes of the M&K translation of the Trilogy.

Speaking before the British House of Commons – a venue strongly suggestive of the Council of Elrond – Reagan said: "If history teaches anything, it teaches that self-delusion in the face of unpleasant facts is folly. […] Let us offer hope. Let us tell the world that a new age is not only possible, but probable."[2]

Speaking at the Council of Elrond, Gandalf said: "It is wisdom to recognize necessity, when all other courses have been weighed, though as folly it may appear to those who cling to false hope." (F. 352) In the council in Aragorn's tents, Gandalf holds out the hope of a new age that Reagan turned into a probability:

> We must walk open-eyed into that trap, with courage, but small hope for ourselves. For, my lords, it may well prove that we ourselves shall perish utterly in a black battle far from the living lands; so that even if Barad-dûr be thrown down, we shall not live to see a new age. But this, I deem, is our duty. And better so than to perish nonetheless – as we surely shall, if we sit here – and know as we die that no new age shall be. (R. 191)

When, after the publication of the M&K abridged translation of Volume I, it became apparent that publication of Volumes II and III would be some time in coming, other unofficial translators stepped in to meet the demand for translations of Volumes II and III, resulting in a 'translation boom' for *LotR*. One key characteristic of the 'boom' translations is that, since they were picking up where M&K left off, they maintained the names and, to some extent, the style of M&K's Volume I.

---

1 Anatolij Moshnitskij, 'Evrazijskie tendentsii v otechestvennoj literature zhanra fentazi', <http://arctogaia.krasu.ru/works/moshnitsky1.shtm>.
2 <http://www.luminet.net/~tgort/empire.htm>.

In the Ukraine, Alina Nemirova came forward. Valeriya Aleksandrovna Matorina, a technical translator, who signs her translations 'VAM', which is the Russian word meaning *for you*, implying, as she herself notes, that her translation is *a gift for you*, did a translation. Sergej L. Koshelev, whose translation of 'Leaf by Niggle' is the most widely reprinted, also did one. N. Estel' – the Tolkien pseudonym for Nadezhda Chertkova – whose translation of *The Silmarillion* has been widely reprinted, was a member of the cohort of the boom as well. Semen Ya. Umanskij, an engineer with a renaissance range of talents, filled in all the blanks in the Bobyr' condensation. In August of 1989, A.I. Alekhin brought out his translation of Volumes II and III – done from Skibniewska's Polish translation[3] as books on tape. In the 1990s, Irina Zabelina, whose translations of Tolkien's minor works like 'Leaf by Niggle' and 'Farmer Giles of Ham', have been published, also did a translation of *LotR* that has yet to be published. The translation of Volumes II and III by Natalya Grigor'eva and Vladimir Grushetskij (G&G), which drew on the Bobyr' condensation without attribution, appeared on the Web, often combined with Gruzberg's translation of Volume I to form a complete digital set of the Trilogy.

3 Perestroika

The translation boom would have been impossible without Perestroika, which reined in the literary strong arm of the State, the Main Directorate for Literary and Publishing Affairs (Glavlit). Glavlit had been established in 1922 to centralize censorship of the press and theatrical arts. Its function was to prohibit the publication and distribution of works containing propaganda against the power of the Soviets, divulging military secrets, inciting public opinion, inciting nationalistic or religious fanaticism or having a pornographic character. It was a political organization and its character changed to match the political ebb and flow of the times; strong under Stalin, relaxed under Khrushchev, tightened again under Brezhnev. Beginning in 1986, Glavlit slowly lost its powers. In 1990, it was reorganized as the Main Directorate for the Protection of Government Secrets in the Press (GUOT) to accent its role in protecting state secrets. As

---

3 Skibniewska, Maria, *Wadca Pierscieni*, Warsaw: Czytelnik Publishers, vol. 1 (*Wyprawa*), 1961; vol. 2 (*Dwie wieze*), 1962; vol. 3 (*Powrót króla*), 1963.

Perestroika took hold, the younger generation felt less and less intimidated. As the power of the Glavlit waned, samizdat lost its impact. The younger generation no longer viewed typescript books as samizdat, but as simply 'unpublished manuscripts'. The change in attitude meant a wider circulation for unofficial views, which sped the process of political change in the Soviet Union. It was under Perestroika that the second, unabridged edition of the M&K translation of Volume I was first published in 1988.

In October 1991, the Glavlit, now GUOT, was finally disbanded, and the publishing boom began. The state-controlled publishing system changed into a market-driven entity almost overnight. Samizdat moved from a bound typescript with six carbon copies to a computer typeset book with thousands of copies. Translations of Tolkien, who is popularly known in Russia as 'The Professor,' were no exception. The full M&K translation came out in 1988, 1990 and 1992. Bobyr's 'adaptation' was published as a single-volume in 1990. The VAM translation came out in 1991, as did the first edition of the full G&G.

4 The Second Publishing Boom

Not quite ten years later, there was a second translation boom. This end of the old millennium and the start of the new saw a burst of new activity. In 1999, a re-telling of *The Lord of the Rings* for children by Yakhnin came on stage. The second revised edition of the full G&G came out in 2000. The M&K translation was not revised, but was widely reprinted. The Gruzberg translation finally was published on CD-ROM. The Kamenkovich and Karrik (K&K) translation, first published in 1994, was republished. A new translation done by Volkovskij appeared in print. And that was just in the year 2000. As 'movie fever' hit Russia, M&K, G&G, K&K and Yakhnin were all reprinted in 2001. In 2002, the Nemirova translation was finally published.

Despite the publishing boom and the 'read-Tolkien-in-the-original' boom, samizdat Tolkien was still alive and well in the new millennium, but it had emigrated to Israel. Alla Khananashvili had taken up the gauntlet of editing Gruzberg's text, which she considered the best of the ones she has read: M&K, G&G, Chertkova and Gruzberg. Her attitude to the available translations of Tolkien was not unique, however. A group of Russian Harry Potter fans, dissatisfied with the published translation, brought out their own version on the Web.

The result of the years of 'exile' in samizdat, and the two publishing booms is that there is not just one published translation of *LotR* in Russia as is common in other countries. There are nine contemporary published translations competing with each other for the reader's attention. Each translator has a slightly different approach to the text. Each translation has a slightly different interpretation of Tolkien. Each translator has a different story to tell. The goal of this paper is to point out the differences.

5 Zinaida Anatol'evna Bobyr'

The condensation and retelling by the well-known science-fiction translator Zinaida Anatol'evna Bobyr' compresses the 3 volumes and 6 books of Tolkien's Trilogy into 1 book, in 3 parts, totaling a mere 486 pages. The table of contents for the first part – Tolkien's volume one – offers a good look at how Bobyr' restructured the original. Bobyr's part one has only 13 chapters, while Tolkien's books one and two total 22 chapters. Bobyr's chapter titles show how her version of the story progresses: 1 - The Ring, 2 - Frodo's Flight, 3 - Strider, 4 - Weathertop, 5 - At the Ford, 6 - Elrond's House, 7 - The Council and Its Decision, 8 - Across the Mountains, 9 - A Journey in the Dark, 10 - On the Bridge at Khazad-Dûm, 11 - In Lorien, 12 - The Great River, 13 - The Company Falls Apart. There are no appendices.

An example of the kind of condensation that it takes to make Tolkien's Trilogy fit into this format can be found in the description of Sam's marriage to Rose. In Bobyr's version, Tolkien's 3 paragraphs (R. 376-377) are pared down to one long sentence. "Sam married Rosie, the girl next door, about whom he had thought even while they were in Mordor, and, at Frodo's request, they moved in with him: there was enough room in the little house for all." (B. 485) Not only does the reader miss Rose's opinion of Sam's going away for a year to help Frodo on his quest ("wasted"), and how well Sam and Rose looked after Frodo (not a Hobbit in the Shire "was looked after with such care"), but Bag End is reduced to a "little house".

At the same time, Bobyr' has elegant translations of seemingly superfluous – in her scheme of things – turns of phrase like the final sentence in her description of the year 1420. "The harvest in the fields, orchards and gardens was unheard of, and no one in the Shire was ill, and everyone was happy and pleased, except those who had to mow the grass." (B. 485) Tolkien's description (R. 375) is, of course, considerably longer, but it ends with "And no one was ill, and everyone was pleased, except those who had to mow the grass."

The same economy of style applies to Bobyr's names. The main characters only have first names, and her approach to the names that she does use is primarily to transliterate them. Bilbo is Бильбо, and Frodo is Фродо, and Sam is Сэм. There is no mention of Baggins, or of Gamgee, or of Bolgers, Boffins or Proudfoot (feet). Place names suffer the same fate. The Shire is Шир [Shir], and The Brandywine is Брендивейн [Brendivejn], and Bree is Бри [Bri], but there is no Hobbiton, Michel Delving or Frogmorton.

There are, however, a few exceptions. Strider is Странник [Strannik]. This is an archaic word for *pilgrim* or *traveler*, and fits well in the style of Tolkien's tale. It is sufficiently far removed from everyday use that the modern reader can easily shift its meaning to include one who wanders, but is not lost. Mirkwood is Чернолес [Chernoles], literally, 'The Dark Forest,' which is a reasonably good calque for Mirkwood. Mount Doom is Гора Ужаса [Gora Uzhasa], 'The Mountain of Terror.' Mount Doom is terrifying, but that is not what Tolkien said. Shadowfax is Быстрокрыл [Bystrokryl], 'Fleet-winged,' which Shadowfax certainly is, but this makes him seem a bit more like Pegasus than Tolkien would probably have liked. All in all, her treatment of the names reflects her treatment of the text: greatly abridged with flashes of skillful wordsmithing.

6 Aleksandr Abramovich Gruzberg

The translation by Aleksandr Abramovich Gruzberg reads somewhat like a gloss of *LotR*. It is firmly rejected by some for its lack of 'style', but others are attracted to it for its attempt at faithfulness to the original, without all the embellishments and intentional changes that can be found in a number of the other translations.

Gruzberg's approach to the names is telling for his approach to the translation of the text. He transliterated most of them. Bilbo Baggins is Бильбо Бэггинс [Bilbo Baggins], Entmoot is Энтмут [Entmoot] and Butterbur is Баттербур [Butterbur]. While there are those Russian readers who find this approach unsatisfactory, it is readily defensible when applied throughout as Gruzberg did. It adds a certain feeling of exoticness to the story for the Russian reader. Leaving the names in transliteration keeps it a very English story.

In a letter to Rayner Unwin Tolkien said:

> *In principle* I object as strongly as is possible to the 'translation' of the *nomenclature* at all (even by a competent person). I wonder why a translator should think himself called on or entitled to do any such thing. That this is an 'imaginary' world does not give him any right to remodel it according to his fancy, even if he could in a few months create a new coherent structure which it took me years to work out. [...] After all the book is English, and by an Englishman, and presumably even those who wish its narrative and dialogue turned into an idiom that they understand, will not ask of a translator that he should deliberately attempt to destroy the local colour. (L. 249-50)

Gruzberg's successes as a translator are best seen in comparison to other versions of the text. In the debate between Gandalf and Erestor at the council of Elrond, Erestor calls the plan to destroy the ring "the path of despair. Of folly I would say, if the long wisdom of Elrond did not forbid me." Gandalf's response rejects the premise of Erestor's argument:

> "Despair, or folly?" said Gandalf. "It is not despair, for despair is only for those who see the end beyond all doubt. We do not. It is wisdom to recognize necessity, when all other courses have been weighed, though as folly it may appear to those who cling to false hope ..." (F. 352)

Gruzberg's rendition of the debate has none of the philosophical divergences of a number of the other translations. Gruzberg's Gandalf says:

> "Despair or insanity?" said Gandalf. "It is not despair: only those despair, who see their inescapable end. We do not despair. It is wisdom to recognize necessity, when all other paths have been weighed, however, to those, who cherish false hope, that wisdom may seem to be insanity."

K&K set out along the other side of a philosophical fault line with their rendition of "see the end beyond all doubt." In K&K's version Gandalf counters Erestor's argument with:

"So it is hopelessness or insanity," rejoined Gandalf. "We are not talking about hopelessness: only those whose end is already predetermined lose hope and despair. Our [end] is not [predetermined]. (K&K, F. 403)

The philosophical fault line that divides K&K and Tolkien is the difference between *predestination* and *foreseeing*. Tolkien does not entirely reject the possibility of foretelling. Galadriel's statement that (italics added) "for all foretelling is *now* vain," implies that at other times foretelling is possible and useful. For Gandalf the decision to be taken is an intellectual exercise to be resolved by the application of wisdom, not the fates. K&K continue their version of Gandalf's speech with an embellished Socratic formulation of the definition of true wisdom, and *necessity* takes a holiday.

> What is true wisdom?* It is, having weighed all the courses of action, picking the only one among them. Perhaps to those who harbor false hopes this indeed seems like insanity.

Their embellishment of the definition of wisdom is not only the addition of the word *true*, which is a loaded word in any Russian philosophical discussion, but also by the addition of a lengthy end note* (K&K, F. 685), which supports their use of *predestination* in Erestor's lines above. They view *true wisdom* as synonymous with "the Northern theory of courage" about which Tolkien wrote in *The Monsters and The Critics*, concluding that "it is necessary to fight to the end, even if victory cannot be counted upon, fight, knowing that the higher powers are fighting on your side and that they too may suffer a defeat in the end." (K&K, F. 685)

M&K make essentially the same – very Russian – interpretation of the debate. In his very verbose argument, M&K's Erestor, too, sees the end of the path that Gandalf proposes beyond all doubt: defeat for them all.

> Elrond is wise, we all know that, and no one would name the only path that leads to victory the path of folly … but at the same time it is impassable and defeat inexorably awaits us. (M&K, F_{1982}. 201; F_{1988}. 333)

This, too, is the philosophy of Ragnarok, which dooms the gods to defeat at the hands of the forces of evil, after which the world will be renewed. M&K's Gandalf instead responds to Erestor with an argument couched in terms of courage and bravery:

> "Defeat inexorably awaits only those who have given themselves over to despair beforehand," countered Gandalf. "To recognize the necessity of a dangerous course of action, when all other paths have been cut off, that is true wisdom." (M&K, F_{1982}. 201; F_{1988}. 333)

For M&K's Gandalf there is no other choice. M&K's Gandalf is accepting the constraints of the situation as the definition of the problem and is reactive. M&K's Gandalf is a fatalist. There is no other choice, therefore we must bravely do as the fates decree. Tolkien's Gandalf believes he has the freedom of action to affect the course of events. The philosophical gap between them is a very wide one.

Volkovskij keeps M&K company with his verbose formulation of this segment by defining the problem in terms of *victory* and *defeat*.

> "So you see it as despair or insanity?" said Gandalf raising his voice. "But is that the case? Despair is the lot of those who have already suffered defeat or see no possibility of victory. But we are not defeated, and know what we have to do. To examine all the possibilities and chose from them the single one that is doable, no matter how dangerous, is not insanity, but wisdom. This decision may seem like insanity to those laboring under the delusion of false hope." (VA&V, F. 374)

In comparison to these versions of the translation, Gruzberg's success can be seen, not in its elegance, but in its reflection of the axiom that doctors follow in treating patients: *First, do no harm.*

Gruzberg's translation is also not without its failures. An example can be found in Tolkien's elaborate phrase from his description of the year 1420. There was a "gleam of beauty beyond that of mortal summers that flicker and pass upon this Middle-earth." (R. 375)

Gruzberg turned this into: "the likes of which mortals are not given to seeing, and which left Middle-earth long ago." This reads too much into "flicker and pass" on Middle-earth. Tolkien is talking about the transitory nature of summer, that stays but a little while, before giving way to fall and winter.

M&K had a much better version: "the likes of which had never been seen before on Middle-earth, where summer flashes only for a brief moment." (M&K, R. 343) Bobyr' had a less elegant, but eminently serviceable: "Everything about

shown with a beauty, the likes of which does not exist in the mortal world."
(B. 485) K&K took the description to a higher ethereal plane with their: "the likes of which are usually beyond conception in mortal lands." (K&K, R. 418) Volkovskij brings the image back down to earth with his "No one in the lands of the mortals inhabiting Middle-earth could remember a summer like this." (V, R. 537) VAM lets her background as a technical translator show through with her: "and left a bright trace of an inexpressible series of years, rolling over the mortal lands of Middle-earth." (VAM, R. 344) In apparent deference to his young audience, Yakhnin avoids all the implications of mortality and immortality with his: "It had been a long time since they had seen such a gentle summer in Hobbitania." (Ya, R. 312) G&G avoided the problem completely, by leaving this sentence out (G&G, R. 333).

At a time when the only other alternative to Tolkien's Trilogy in Russian was Bobyr's abridged version, Gruzberg's samizdat translation was a major accomplishment of daring in the hostile environment of media censorship in the Soviet Union.

7 Vladimir Sergeevich Murav'ev and Andrej Andreevich Kistyakovskij

The translation by Vladimir Murav'ev and Andrej Kistyakovskij is a very much russified version of Tolkien's Trilogy.

Kistyakovskij's names are indicative of the degree to which M&K adapted Tolkien to the Russian intellectual climate. While *Bilbo* remained Бильбо [Bilbo] in Russian, *Baggins* turned into Торбинс [Torbins], quite literally, *bag* (торба [torba]) + -ins. *Boffin* became Булкинс [Bulkins], from булка [bulka], *dinner roll*. Sandyman turned into Пескунс [Peskuns], based on песок [pesok], *sand*.

In the introduction to the second, unabridged edition of the first book of the trilogy, refuting all Tolkien's protestations to the contrary (L. 158n, L. 406-7), Murav'ev provides an etymology of the word *hobbit* as: "*ho(mo)* [Latin for *man*] + *(ra)bbit*." (M&K2, I. 20) Following the etymology that Murav'ev gives for the word *Hobbit*, Kistyakovskij made up names for the three strains of Hobbits all based on associations with *rabbits* or *hares*. The Fallohides changed into Беляки [Belyaki], the Russian word for *white hare*. The Stoors became Струсы [Strusy], derived from the verb *to cower* струсить [strusit'], a characteristic so typical for a rabbit that it is part of the Latin name for rabbits (*Lepus Timidus*), as well as the descriptor for the hare in Fangorn's list of Living Creatures. (T. 84) The Harfoots turned into Лапитупы [Lapitupy], based on the name of a character in a novella by Yurij Olesha (1899-1960) entitled Три толстяка [The Three Fat Men],[4] in which Olesha uses animals to describe the characters. Lapitup was the circus strongman and, when he did his act, his "muscles moved under his skin, exactly like rabbits that had been swallowed by a boa constrictor."

Kistyakovskij's accent on the '(ra)bbit' in Hobbit does not stop there. Based on the words for *rabbit* (кролик [krolik]) and for *hare* (зайчик [zajchik]) he builds a whole family of '(ra)bbit' names. Bandobras Took becomes Бандобрас Крол [Bandobras Krol]; Tookland, Укролье [Ukrol'e], literally *Rabbit-land*; and Tuckborough, Укрольные Низины [Ukrol'nye Niziny], literally the *Rabbit-land Lowlands*. Crickhollow, where Frodo moved before going on his quest, becomes Кроличья Балка [Krolich'ya Balka], literally *Rabbit Hollow*. Buckland becomes Заячьи Холмы [Zayach'i Kholmy], literally *Hare Hills*; Buckelbury is Зайгород [Zajgorod], literally *Hare-town*; and the Brandybucks are Брендизайки [Brendizajki], read as the *Brandy-hares*.

Both Murav'ev and Kistyakovskij have an excellent command of Russian and their literary skill shows through in the text. This is a major positive factor for them in any comparison with the other translators. At the same time, it is a major negative factor for them in any comparison with the original.

M&K's text, in general, as is typical of Russian literature, is much more full of doom and gloom than Tolkien's. In Chapter 8 of Book IV ('The Stairs of Cirith Ungol'), for example, the narrator describes what Frodo, Sam and Gollum "expected would be their last meal before they went down into the Nameless Land, maybe the last meal they would ever eat together." (T. 406) While all the other translators manage to capture the idea behind Tolkien's phrase, M&K turn it into "maybe even the last meal of their lives" [может, и последнюю (трапезу) в жизни] (M&K, T. 378), which is much more somber than Tolkien.

---

4 Yurij Olesha. *Povesti i rasskazy*, Moscow: 'Khudozhestvennaya literatura', 1965, pp. 121-238.

The parallels between Chapter 8 of Book VI ('The Scouring of the Shire') and early Soviet history are readily apparent to any student of the Soviet period. During the Soviet period, this chapter by itself could have been enough to put *LotR* on the Soviet censors' list of banned books. M&K did not make things any easier for the censors with their rendition of this chapter, which is filled with loaded words from the Soviet era.

Their rendition of the passage in which the leader of the Shirriffs tells Frodo to come along quietly is overflowing with them in a heavily stylized parody of the jargon of secret police arrests and the show trials of the mid-1930s. (Italics added)

> Sir, sir, bethink yourself. In accordance with the *Generalissimo's* personal orders you are required, immediately and without the least resistance, to proceed under our *armed escort* to Bywater, where you will be handed over to the *secret police*. When the *Generalissimo* pronounces sentence in your case, then they may give you a chance to speak. And if you do not want to spend the rest of your life in the *Correctional-Labor Burrows*, then my advice to you is: bite your tongues. (M&K, R. 314-315)

M&K's imitation of a Russian policeman making an arrest is an elegant equal to Tolkien's replication of an English bobby in the performance of his duty. Both are the stuff of stage, screen and literature. The reader could identify the speaker as a policeman simply from the flow of the words, even if the speaker was not identified in the text. The loaded words in M&K's version, however, give this passage a more sinister, specifically Soviet context.

The most obvious of these is *Generalissimo* [Генералиссимус]. There was only one Generalissimo in the Soviet Union and that was Stalin. For those who might have missed the implication of *Generalissimo* as the translation for *Chief*, M&K followed Tolkien's shift to a new sobriquet for the Chief a few pages later with another loaded word in the same vein. In the episode that sees the first casualties of the Rebellion fall, the leader of the ruffians who have come to restore order, says: "The Boss is losing his temper." (R. 358) M&K render the word *Boss* with Вождь [Vozhd'] (M&K, R. 326), which is the other more commonly recognized sobriquet for Stalin. This word is so loaded in the context of this chapter that none of the other translators dared use it here even though it is the most direct translation of *Boss*.

8 Valeriya Aleksandrovna Matorina (VAM)

Matorina's translation is really an adaptation, like the translations of Shakespeare into modern English that are used in high schools. There is clearly a need for this kind of adaptation in English, since, as Nancy Martsch pointed out in her review[5] of Peter Jackson's movie version of *The Fellowship of the Ring*, those of us who are long-time Tolkien fans tend to forget what a large and varied vocabulary Tolkien has. Those whose command of English is poor for one reason or another find Tolkien difficult to read. In her article, Martsch quotes one such reader: "I tried to read the book once before, after reading *The Hobbit*, but it was too hard to understand. Now [after the movie] I know what it is about, I will try again."

VAM's translation has never been fully appreciated in Russia. It has not been reprinted since its first printing in 1991. It was, however, appreciated by K&K, who used it as a crib for their translation. This can be clearly seen in the Chapter 'The Battle of the Pelenor Fields', in the segment in which Eomer "cast his sword up in the sunlight and sang as he caught it" (R. 150), out of joy at seeing the standard with the signs of Elendil unfurl. All the translators – except Yakhnin, VAM and K&K – had Eomer toss his sword up into the air and catch it again, using the same verb подбросить [podbrosit']. VAM and K&K, on the other hand, had Eomer lift up his blade so that it caught the sunlight. Their phrasing is the same, with the exception of one (additional) word, typical of K&K's verbosity. Лезвие (ослепительно) засверкало на солнце. [Lezvie (oslepitel'no) zasverkalo na solntse] (K&K, R. 161, VAM, R. 134) They could not both have taken the same wrong turn by coincidence. Yakhnin, true to form, left out this segment.

VAM's Hobbit names are often transparent translations. Butterbur is named Медовар [Medovar], literally, *Mead-brewer*. Bullroarer is Бычеглас [Bycheglas], *Bull's voice*. Bracegirdle is Тугобрюх [Tugobryukh], meaning *tight belly*. Cotton is Норкинс [Norkins], a combination of *hole* нора [nora] + -ins. Brownlock is Буркинс [Burkins], from *brown* (бурый [buryj]) + -ins. Headstrong is Строптивинс [Stroptivins], which echoes Shakespeare's *The Taming of the*

---

[5] *Beyond Bree*, March 2002, p. 5.

Shrew (Укрощение строптивой [Ukroshchenie stroptivoj]) + -ins. Whitfoot is Белоног [Belonog], which means *White-foot*. Wingfoot is *Flighted One* (Летучник [Letuchnik]). And, of course, her characteristic Хоббитшир [Khobbitshir] (Hobbit + Shire), on the analogy of all the English place names that end in -shire, like Oxfordshire, Devonshire and Cheshire. An unattributed map with her names is included with the 'Olimp' Press edition[6] (1993) of the M&K translation. It is immediately recognizable as hers by the title box in the upper right corner of the map: Хоббитшир [Khobbitshir]. The map of Middle-earth in this edition is hers as well.[7]

A brief look in the 'Prologue' is sufficient for a sample of the vocabulary that is hard to understand in *The Lord of the Rings*. The meaning of some words in Tolkien's extensive vocabulary can be elusive not only for some readers, but also for some of the translators. In the 'Prologue', Tolkien says that the Hobbits' "elusiveness is due solely to a professional skill that heredity and practice, and a close friendship with the earth, have rendered inimitable by bigger and clumsier races." (F. 20) VAM says that "the Hobbits never studied magic, they simply grew to be one with the earth, and their ability to slip away is a hereditary characteristic, sharpened by practice to a perfection that is unattainable for their large and clumsy neighbors." This is a challenging sentence, but VAM's rendition of it is quite readable.

Gruzberg's translation replicated *elusiveness*, but *inimitable* eluded him. "In reality, the Hobbits never practiced magic, and their elusiveness is a result of an inherited skill developed with practice, and of their friendship with nature, which repays them in a way that the larger and more clumsy races cannot even imagine." His rendition, is, nevertheless, readable and unembellished.

G&G followed Gruzberg verbosely, the only other translators to replicate *elusiveness*. "In reality, of course, the Hobbits did not know any magic at all, and were exclusively indebted for their elusiveness to a masterful skill, based on a respectful attitude towards tradition, a lot of practice and a close friendship with the earth, that is uncharacteristic of and incomprehensible for clumsy Big Folk." (G&G, F. 10)

---

6 *Vlastelin Kolets: Letopis' vtoraya i tret'ya*, Baku: 'Olimp', 1993, pp. 4-5.
7 *Vlastelin Kolets: Letopis' pervaya*, Baku: 'Olimp', 1993, pp. 102-103.

Elusiveness eluded Nemirova, but she deftly replicated *inimitable*. She said: "In reality, the Hobbits never practiced magic and only achieved all this through good training; hereditary skills, unceasing practice and a closeness to the earth make them inimitable for tall and clumsy tribes." (N, F. 10) Her version is very close to Tolkien's stylistically, though it is spoiled by her clumsy use of the pronoun *all*.

K&K had a much more verbose rendition of *elusiveness*. Instead of VAM's 2 words, they had 5: "the art of disappearing from in front of your eyes," and they did not even attempt a translation of "have rendered inimitable by bigger and clumsier races." "In reality, the Hobbits never practiced magic; they were simply closely tied to nature, and usually achieved a high [level of] professionalism in the art of disappearing from in front of your eyes, which, in part, was imbibed with their mother's milk, and, in part, sharpened with daily training." (K&K, F. 18)

The inimitably literary M&K got straight to the point with: "The hobbits did not have any idea of magic at all; from birth they are masters at hiding. The minute anything happens they can disappear from sight, to the amazement of their bigger and clumsy neighbors." (M&K, F. 32) Theirs is a well-formed, easy-to-read sentence, despite what it leaves out.

Volkovskij brings this sentence 'down to earth' with a colloquial style that, while readable and understandable, gives Tolkien a whole new feel. "Hobbits have never ever had anything to do with any magic: it is a skill in their blood that is kept up by practice, as well as by a friendly closeness with the earth, that is unattainable by clumsy Big Folk." (V, F. 14)

9 Natalya Grigor'eva and Vladimir Grushetskij

Grigor'eva and Grushetskij (G&G) have an enthusiastic following, who avidly recommend this translation above all others. Feelings run high in Russia about which translation is the best. One Russian personal web page, on which the page-owner lists his favorite books, posts a warning to readers. "Do not under any circumstances read the Murav'ev translation (the bookstores have been flooded with them), and especially not the 'retelling for children' (the compiler of which is a certain L. Yakhnin). That is harmful not only to your mental and physical (you will be beat up, if you quote [from them]) health, but also to that of those around you."[8]

G&G's translation, however, introduces a certain subtle philosophical shift into Tolkien's tale. For example, in Chapter 2 of Book V, 'The Passing of the Grey Company', in which Isildur lays a curse on the king of the Men of the Mountain, Isildur says: "And if the West prove mightier than thy Black Master, this curse I lay upon thee and thy folk: to rest never until your oath is fulfilled." (R. 64) In G&G's version of the curse, there is no conditional clause. G&G's Isildur says: "The West is stronger than your Black Master." (G&G, T. 46) The omission of that one word changes the import of the entire text. If the West is without a doubt greater, as G&G's Isildur states, then there is no suspense in the story. The West will certainly win. That is not the case in Tolkien's tale. Tolkien always admits the possibility of defeat.

In the same chapter, Aragorn describes how he claimed his right to the Stone of Orthanc, and in doing so revealed himself to the Black Lord. In comparison to the original, the speech that G&G's Aragorn makes is conspicuous by its omissions. (Omissions are in italics in the quote of the original below.)

> "You forgot to whom you speak," said Aragorn *sternly*, and his eyes glinted. "*Did I not openly proclaim my title before the deson of Edoras?* What do you fear that I should say to him? *Nay, Gimli," he said in a softer voice, and* the grimness left his face, and he looked like one who has laboured *in sleepless pain for many nights.* "Nay, *my friends,* I am the lawful master of the Stone, and I had *both* the right *and the strength* to use it, *or so I judged.* The right cannot be doubted. The strength was enough – barely."
>
> He drew a deep breath. "It was a bitter struggle, *and the weariness is slow to pass.* I spoke no word to him, and in the end I wrenched the Stone to my own will. That alone he will find hard to endure. And he beheld me. Yes, Master Gimli, he saw me, but in other guise than you see me here. *If that will aid him, then I have done ill. But I do not think so.* To know that I lived *and walked the earth* was a blow *to his heart, I deem*; for he knew it not till now. *The eyes in Orthanc did not see through the armour of Theoden; but* Sauron has not forgotten Isildur and the sword of Elendil. Now in the very hour of his great designs the heir of Isildur and the Sword are revealed; *for I showed the blade re-forged to him.* He is not so mighty *yet* that he is above fear; nay, doubt ever gnaws him." (R. 62-63; G&G, R. 44-45)

---

8 <http://ivbespalov.chat.ru/library.htm>, 23 January, 2002.

The omissions give the text another voice, especially the omissions of "or so I judged", "If that will aid him, then I have done ill. But I do not think so," and "I deem." These phrases of self-depreciation, show that Aragorn does not consider himself infallible. Without them, in G&G's text, he is a much stronger, more arrogant figure.

G&G's text is not, however, without its own verbose eloquence, as can clearly be seen in the back translation of their version of the second paragraph from the segment above.

> A shudder passed across the Ranger's face. "It was a bitter struggle, but, not only did I not say anything to him, but I also wrenched the Palantir from his control. That was a blow to him, a heavy blow. And what's more, the Enemy saw me. Yes, Worthy Gimli, he saw me, but not in the guise in which I am known to you. Up until now, he did not know of my existence, and that was a second blow. Saruman in Orthanc simply saw a man in the livery of Rohan, but Sauron has forgotten neither Isildur nor Narsil, and now, at this difficult time for the Enemy, he beheld Isildur's heir, saw Anduril and recognized the sword. No matter how great his power, even he knows fear, and worries ever gnaw him." (G&G, R. 44-45)

The embellishments demonstrate G&G's grasp of Tolkien's names: The Stone is indeed one of the Palantir. Narsil is the name of Elendil's sword forged by Telchar in the First Age and broken in the battle with Sauron. Isildur cut the One Ring from Sauron's finger with the part of the blade remaining on the hilt. When the sword was re-forged, it was renamed Anduril, the Flame of the West. Name dropping like this does not really make G&G more Tolkien-like, but it does cover up for philosophical shifts like the one in the last sentence of the paragraph. Tolkien says that there will come a point at which Sauron no longer feels fear. G&G's closing sentence leaves out the threat of that change.

Interestingly, there are a number of instances, in which G&G's translation matches Bobyr's word for word for whole sentences. Unfortunately, the segment above was not one of them. Bobyr' got the last sentence right. (B. 340) There were more such coincidences of the text in the samizdat version that was available as a file on the net, but enough of them made it into print to still be noticeable to those with only the print version to compare.

A good example can be found in Chapter 5 of Book IV, 'The Window on the West', in which Faramir is interrogating Frodo, and Sam steps forward to confront

Faramir in Frodo's defense. (T. 345-346; G&G, T. 258; B. 207) The texts are not identical, but there are enough sentences with formulations that uniquely deviate from the original, that are replicated word for word, to show that they share a common heritage. As the segment begins, for example, "bursting into the middle of the ring, he [Tolkien's Sam] strode up to his master's side." (T. 345) G&G/Bobyr's Sam, however, "jumped up, and in two skips was by his friend's side." (G&G, T. 258; B. 207) When Faramir puts Sam in his place, Tolkien's Sam "sat down heavily with a red face." (T. 346) G&G/Bobyr's Sam, however, "turned red up to his ears, and did as he was told." The rest of this paragraph is word for word the same with one exception. Bobyr' uses the plural word for *news* (вести [vesti]), while G&G use the singular (весть [vest']) (G&G, T. 258; B. 207).

G&G would have been better off to pay more attention to Bobyr'. Bobyr's rendition of Faramir's rebuke to Sam is much better. Tolkien's Faramir says: "Do not speak before your master, whose wit is greater than yours," which Bobyr' translates as: "Do not talk like that in the presence of your friend, who is, of course, wiser than you." G&G's Faramir instead says "Your friend, I think, is no stupider than you, so give him a chance to speak for himself." Tolkien's and Bobyr's Faramir is the classic definition of a gentleman, who never insults someone unintentionally, because he says that Frodo is wiser than Sam. G&G's Faramir is less polite, because he says that Frodo is no stupider than Sam. Any statement using the word stupid is always open to (mis)interpretation as an insult.

As he closes his rebuke to Sam, Tolkien's Faramir says: "I do not slay needlessly ... Neither do I talk in vain." Bobyr's Faramir does not slay needlessly, and "does not talk unnecessarily," which is a reasonably good match. G&G's Faramir, however, does not slay needlessly, and "answers for his words," which is not an explanation of why he is questioning Frodo, but a statement of fact about his character.

10 Mariya Kamenkovich (née Trofimchik) and Valerij Karrik

The translation by Kamenkovich and Karrik (the pseudonym under which Mariya's husband Valerij writes) is a fully annotated academic edition. The annotations generally represent good scholarship and are informative.

A good example of their annotations is their end note for the name *Baggins*.

> As is known from *The Hobbit*, Bilbo Baggins loved to drink tea at four o'clock in the afternoon, i.e. between the traditional English lunch and 'five-o'clock tea'. This significant detail was not included by accident. In some rural areas of England, notes the Oxford English dictionary, which Shippey cites (p. 56), four-o'clock tea was well known, under the name no less of *baggins*. [...] This dialectical meaning of the word baggins carries with it a number of associations. Bilbo is very much like his name: he is decidedly prosaic, he is a typical representative of the middle class, does not avoid rural customs and does not pretend to be an aristocrat, as do his relatives the Sackville-Bagginses. He is generous, prosperous, does not deny himself the simple pleasures, is conservative, old-fashioned (*baggins* is undoubtedly an old-fashioned custom!), a devotee of rural life. In Shippey's words, it is precisely due to these characteristics that Bilbo can successfully fill his role as the "link" between the world of heroic epos and the modern reader: he simultaneously belongs to our world – according to Shippey, he is a typical, modern, rural 'bourgeois' – and to the ancient world (what else is Bilbo except an old-English farmer?). (K&K, H. 312-13)

K&K's style is generally verbose. In explaining the police state that was instituted in the Shire during Frodo's absence, Tolkien's Farmer Cotton says: "if anyone got 'uppish' as they called it, they followed" the Mayor to the Lockholes. (R. 360) K&K hedged their bets by using two colloquial verbs to better define the concept of 'uppishness' to the Russian reader. Their version reads: "began 'to get too proud' or 'to stick out'" [«заноситься» или «высовываться»] (K&K, R. 401).

This verbosity gives their text a somewhat heavy feeling. For example, the name of the Ring from Elrond's tale of the Elven-Smiths of Eregion, was "the One Ring to be their master." (F. 318) K&K's version is: "the One Ring, with the help of which he hoped to enslave them" [с помощью которого надеялся поработить их]. (KK&S, F. 363) The idea behind Tolkien's words is there, but the expression of the idea lacks elegance.

K&K, however, occasionally make subtle changes to Tolkien's text. Hope – a key tenant of Christianity – plays a central role in Tolkien's story. It is a major structural element in his worldview. The whole of Frodo's quest is built on hope. Tolkien makes this clear in Chapter 8 of Book II of *The Fellowship of the Ring*, in a conversation between Galadriel and Gimli, in which Galadriel says: "I do not foretell, for all foretelling is now vain: on the one hand lies darkness, and on the other only hope." (F. 487) K&K's rendition changes only from an adverb to an adjective, which changes Galadriel's statement from a philosophical one into a mere statement of fact. "[...] on the one hand darkness, on the other only one hope [единственная надежда]." (K&K, F. 552) This interpretation of *only hope* as *only one hope* is supported by the story line. Destroying the Ring is the only hope of success. The change, however, makes *hope* specific, robbing Galadriel's statement of its universality. None of the other translators – except M&K – had trouble with the formulation of this part of the clause. M&K's version did not contain either of the two uses of *hope* in the original. (M&K, F_{1982}. 300; F_{1988}. 463) Their viewpoint is one of fatalism, which is one of the things that makes M&K's tale so very typically Russian.

11 Vitalij Volkovskij

The translation by Volkovskij shows a good deal of imagination; too much, perhaps. Most of his imagination is shown in his skillful embellishments. It can be seen in his treatment of *Baggins* and *Bag End*. He did not translate Baggins like Kistyakovskij and G&G, or transliterate it like the other translators. He invented a brand new, non-sense word, and told the reader what it means in a pair of very well-done embellishments to the 'Prologue'. The first is to the last paragraph of 'On Finding the Ring' (Embellishment emphasized in italics. Compare JRRT: P. 35-36).

> Bilbo returned to his *estate, which is called Beben' (an interesting, obviously old hobbit word – since time immemorial this has been the word used for a back bag)*, in the fifty-second year of his life, 22 June 1342 S.R., and from that point nothing notable occurred in the Shire until in 1401 he prepared to celebrate his hundred-and-eleventh birthday. It is here that our history begins. (V, P. 32)

Volkovskij continues establishing the pedigree for the word бебень [beben'] in his embellishment to the 'Note on the Shire Records', in which Tolkien lists Meriadoc's publications. One of these is called *Old Words and Names in the Shire*. In the original, the book shows Meriadoc's "special interest in discovering the kinship with the language of the Rohirrim of such 'shire-words' as *mathom* and old elements in place names." (P. 39) In Volkovskij's version (V, I. 34), the book examined the derivation of ancient words like «мутень» [muten'] (*mathom*) and «бебень» [beben'], which he set off in inverted commas. This squarely places the new name for *Bag End*, and, by implication, Volkovskij's new name for *Baggins* (Беббинс [Bebbins]) in the category of 'shire-words' like *mathom*, which Tolkien had introduced several pages earlier (P. 25).

Volkovskij has lots of names with the same ending to increase the feeling of depth for his linguistic illusion that бебень [beben'] and мутень [muten'] are old 'shire-words'. His names for the *Stoors* and *Fallohides* both end in -ень [-en'] in the singular: Схватень [Skhvaten'] and Скрытень [Skryten'], as does his version of the nickname for Hamfast Gamgee: Gaffer (Старбень [Starben']). The first part of the nickname Gaffer, Стар [Star], is readily recognizable to the reader as the root of the adjective for *old*: старый [staryj]. This hints that the names can be analyzed linguistically, and the meaning of мутень [muten'] suddenly becomes clear. It is derived from the adjective мутный [mutnyj], which means *unclear, confused, vague*.

Volkovskij's version of *Fallohide* (Скрытни [Skrytni, pl.]) can also be analyzed linguistically, but the analysis says more about Volkovskij than it does about the Fallohides. His name is based on the root скрыть [skryt'], which means *to hide* or *to conceal*. It could best be translated as *the hidden ones*. This interpretation is supported by Volkovskij's final sentence in the paragraph describing the Fallohides, which bears but faint resemblance to what Tolkien said in the original.

> Dig deeper into the family tree of any prominent family and you will probably bump into a 'hidden one': the Tooks came from them as well as the Masters of Buckland. (V, P. 17)

> JRRT: Even in Bilbo's time the strong Fallohidish strain could still be noted among the greater families, such as the Tooks and the Masters of Buckland. (P. 22)

If one has to dig deeper into a family tree to find a Fallohidish strain, then it must have been hidden. In Tolkien's version, no effort was needed to note it among the greater families of the Shire. Volkovskij apparently made a translation mistake, and adjusted the text to make his interpretation fit. He appears to have been confused by the homonyms *hide* as in *to conceal*, and *hide* as in *the skin of an animal*.

Yet another interesting embellishment is Volkovskij's verbose rendition of the tale of the Elven Smiths told at the Council of Elrond. In Volkovskij's version, it is a tale of:

> the Elven-Smiths of Eregion who lived in close friendship with the dwarves of Moria, of elves who were doomed by their uncontrollable craving for knowledge. At that time Sauron had not yet become the visible embodiment of evil: his countenance was fair and his speech seductive. He offered the elves his help and, in fact, taught them much, but he did this only so that he could treacherously (вероломно [verolomno]) learn their most treasured secrets. Having gained what he desired, in the furnace of the Fiery Mountain Sauron forged the All-powerful Ring, which was supposed to give him power over all the magic Rings of the elves. (V, F. 333)

> [Compare JRRT:] of the Elven-smiths of Eregion and their friendship with Moria, and their eagerness for knowledge, by which Sauron ensnared them. For in that time he was not yet evil to behold, and they received his aid and grew mighty in craft, whereas he learned all their secrets, and betrayed them, and forged secretly in the Mountain of Fire the One Ring to be their master. (F. 318)

For the Soviet reader, the key word here is вероломно [verolomno], which is normally translated as *treacherously*, or *faithlessly*, but literally means 'breaking faith'. The use of this word is commonly associated with Nazi-Germany's attack on the Soviet Union in June of 1941. Almost every Russian Soviet-era history of World War II begins its description of the Nazi-German attack with this word. For the Soviet reader the use of this word in this context invokes an image as familiar as the "day that will live in infamy" from Roosevelt's speech following the Japanese attack on Pearl Harbor.

12 Leonid Yakhnin

The translation by Leonid Yakhnin, a well-known children's writer, is a retelling for children. It has the same characters and brief glimpses of the text of Tolkien's trilogy, but, on the whole, it is a different tale, in a different style, for a different audience.

It is very much abridged. The table of contents for the first volume offers a good look at how Yakhnin has restructured Tolkien's original. Yakhnin's volume one is one book with 17 chapters. Tolkien's volume one is two books with 12 and with 10 chapters respectively. Yakhnin's chapter titles show how his version of the story progresses: Prologue, 1 - The Disappearance, 2 - The Secret Conversation, 3 - The Black Rider, 4 - Four Hobbits, 5 - Tom Bombadil, 6 - The Darkness of the Barrow, 7 - Strider, 8 - The Ghost Strikes, 9 - The White Knight, 10 - Эльфорт [Elf-ort] (Rivendell), 11 - The Council, 12 - The Journey to the Crimson Gates, 13 - In the Caves of Moria, 14 - The Terror of the Deep, 15 - The Golden Forest, 16 - The Empress of the Elves, 17 - Parting. There are no appendices.

Yakhnin's Prologue is shortened into the briefest (5 pages) summary of *The Hobbit* and an explanation of what a Hobbit is. It ends with a comment about Bilbo that is out of character for Tolkien's Bilbo, and more reminiscent of the Russian Hobbit knock-offs by Dmitrij Suslin.[9] Yakhnin ends the Prologue with: "His [Bilbo's] life would have gone on like this, surrounded by good neighbors and relations, but the irrepressible Bilbo Baggins was not like that. He had grown tired of the peaceful life." (Y, F. 11) This is a great lead-in for Suslin's adventures of Bilbo series, but it is not what Tolkien had in mind as the reason that Bilbo left The Shire. Tolkien's Bilbo needs a holiday. He feels old and stretched out like too little butter spread over too much bread. He is looking for peace and quiet so he can rest (F. 58).

Bilbo's classic, long (3 pages) speech at his birthday party (F. 54) is shortened into a little more than three sentences. "My Friends! Dear close relatives and distant relations, nearby neighbors and those who have come from the far marches, I am happy to see you all in my home. You have eaten and drunk to my health, not sparing your stomachs, enough so that it should last me another 111 years. I will be sure to take your well wishes with me when I go." (Y, F. 21-22) With which Yakhnin's Bilbo disappears. This is typical for Yakhnin's style, for his is not really a translation – though it says so on the title page – but a retelling for children, full of vivid details that speak to a

---

9 Dmitrij Yu. Suslin. *Khobbit i Gendal'f* [*The Hobbit and Gandalf*], Moscow: Armada, 2000.

child's imagination, but short on long speeches, which children inevitably find boring.

On the other hand, Yakhnin's eloquent narrator knows how to embellish Tolkien's text when he feels like it. The image of Bilbo in his office just before Gandalf's arrival in the first chapter, is a good example.

> And so, Bilbo Baggins was sitting in his office, smoking a pipe and thinking about how he would leave, right after the party, following the trail of his old journey and past adventures, reviving his youth to find a quiet place where no one would keep him from dreaming sweat dreams and recalling pleasant memories. He would open the magical box of his memory with the secret key that only he knew about, and, like a conjurer, would pull out the long ribbon of years and turn them into the pages of a book, which would certainly end with the words: '... lived long and happily and finished his days ...' No, perhaps like this: '... and his days passed peacefully and freely to the very end ...' Eh, no, this would be better: 'lived very long and happily and ...' (Y, F. 15)

Bilbo is talking out loud to himself at this point and is surprised when Gandalf makes his entrance to the scene, finishing Bilbo's last sentence for him. This is a marvelous image, but it is Yakhnin and not Tolkien.

The subtle philosophical nuances of Tolkien's text that are the principal challenge to the translator hold no fear for Yakhnin, because he does not even try to deal with them. As Tolkien's Treebeard recites the old list in search of the Hobbits' place in this cosmology, he cannot find them, and Merry suggests that he add a new line. "We always seem to have got left out of the old lists, and the old stories," said Merry, without even guile enough to hide his own right name, which amazes Treebeard (T. 85).

Yakhnin's Treebeard says that he cannot remember how the list goes any further, and Yakhnin's Pippin takes advantage of this weakness to trick him. With a wink to Merry, he tells Treebeard "cunningly" that: "You missed us. We come right after the dwarves. Don't you remember?" (Y, T. 53) It is bad enough that they play tricks on Treebeard, whose trust is key to the story, but the 'forgotten' line they give him for the list is much too boastful for a real Hobbit. It is "Hobbits, the brave hole-dwellers." (Y, T. 54) Tolkien's line was the considerably less pretentious: "Half-grown hobbits, the hole-dwellers." (T. 85)

As the story of the Third Age draws to a close with the departure of the Wise, the Elves and the Ringbearers from Middle-earth, Sam once again meets the lady Galadriel, and Tolkien has her say: "I hear and see that you [Sam] have used my gift well. The Shire shall now be more than ever blessed and beloved." (R. 382) Yakhnin's Galadriel makes a different pronouncement. "I know, Master Samwise, that you used my gift well. Now happiness and love have settled into the Shire forever." (Y, R. 321) This is the 'happy-ever-after' fairy tale ending that Yakhnin's Bilbo was struggling to find as the tale begins. The end to Bilbo's book in Tolkien's version was "and he lived happily ever after to the end of his days." (F. 58) Forever is a long time. Tolkien was not quite that sure of his ability to tell the future.

13 Alina V. Nemirova

The cover blurb for the Nemirova translation calls this a 'new' translation, but that is a relative term. It is new to print (2002), but her samizdat translation circulated in the mid-1980s. The blurb also praises her translation for not having annotations or embellishments, something that not all the other translations can brag about.

Her names are an interesting mix of Kistyakovskij and her own inventiveness. Baggins, for example, is Торбинс [Torbins], The Shire is Хоббитания [Khobbitaniya] and Rohan is Ристания [Ristaniya], all vintage Kistyakovskij. In her introduction, Nemirova says that offering alternatives to those of Kistyakovskij's names that she kept would be like trying to give Don Quixote or Paris another name. Her own names range from the successful Бригор [Brigor] (Bree) and Великие Норы [Velikie Nory] (Michel Delving), to the less elegant Сэм Джемджи [Sem Dzhemdzhi] (Sam Gamgee) and Шерстон [Sherston] (Cotton).

Brigor is an inventive Celtic-Russian tautology [Bree + gor(a)] on the basis of Tolkien's example of Brill, derived from Bree (Celtic/Welsh) + (h)ill (English) (TC. 190), which Tolkien uses to explain the origin of the name Bree. Velikie Nory, literally 'Great Holes' is a transparent translation of Michel Delving. Her Russian spelling of Sam Gamgee, however, assumes that Sam's last name is pronounced as [jemjee], and her rendition of Farmer Cotton's last name is only slightly better than G&G's name in the samizdat edition of their translation. There they based their name (Хлопчатник [Khlopchatnik]) on the Russian word for *cotton* (the textile material), хлопок [khlopok], against Tolkien's specific instructions to the contrary. (TC. 174) Tolkien said that *Cotton* was originally a place name, based on *cot(tage)* + *tun* (Old English for village), literally 'a village of cottages'. Nemirova bases her name for *Cotton* on the Russian word for *wool*, шерсть [sherst'].

Nemirova's is a solid translation, which ably deals with most of the subtleties of the conversation between Gandalf and Bilbo, in which Gandalf asks, if Bilbo means to go on with his plan. (F. 49) The sequence of actions and the possibility that Bilbo might change his mind are important, and most of the other translators took one or another philosophical detour here. Nemirova got these nuances right, but left out one key word: *hope*. Tolkien's Gandalf says: "Stick to your plan – your whole plan, mind – and I hope it will turn out for the best, for you, and for all of us." (F. 49) Nemirova's Gandalf says: "and everything will turn out better for you and for all of us." (N, F. 35) The loss of this one word makes Gandalf seem more sure of himself than he is. Gandalf cannot foretell the outcome of their actions. He can only hope that what they are about to do is the right choice. Only K&K, Aleksandrova and Volkovskij used the word *hope* in this line of Gandalf's conversation with Bilbo. Abandoning *hope* is a very great misstep in Tolkien's scheme of things.

In Saruman's temptation of Gandalf, Tolkien's Saruman said: "We can bide our time, we can keep our thoughts in our hearts, deploring maybe evils done by the way, but approving the high and ultimate purpose: Knowledge, Rule, Order." (F. 340) Nemirova has an excellent translation of the sentence leading up to the ultimate purpose, but the three words defining the ultimate purpose were a special challenge to all the translators, especially the word in the middle: *Rule*. Nemirova, G&G, Volkovskij and Aleksandrova, all chose the word *Power* Власть [Vlast'] as their version of *Rule*.

"Power," said Tolkien, is "an ominous and sinister word in all the tales, except when applied to the gods." (L. 152) In an inducement to Gandalf to join

Sauron, the word *Power* oversteps its mark and is not credible as a temptation to Gandalf. Since Sauron was well-known for the power of his words, they would have been carefully chosen for the best effect. *Power* is what he might have thought, but not what he would have said.

Some of the other translators took another tact with the word *rule*. It can also call to mind the *rule of law*, especially when followed by *order*, as in *law and order*. This was the approach taken by K&K, VAM and Gruzberg. K&K and VAM translated *Rule* as *Law* (statute) [Закон]. (K&K, F. 388) Gruzberg chose *Law* (system of justice) [право] as in *Law and Order* [правопорядок].

M&K had two different versions of the three goals. Both are major deviations from Tolkien's text. In their first edition (1982), the goals were 'Wisdom, the General Welfare and Order' [Мудрость, Всеобщее Благоденствие и Порядок] (M&K, F_{1982}. 191). The goals are as admirable as any that could be advanced for society. In M&K's second edition (1988) on the eve of the fall of Communism, the three goals have changed. They are 'Omniscience, Despotism and Order' [Всезнание, Самовластие и Порядок] (M&K, F_{1988}. 320). This is Saruman's goal of 'Knowledge, Rule and Order' taken to its extreme. Here the would-be Ring bearer clearly resembles the despotic Stalin, who knew it all and maintained order with an iron hand.

The Russian word Всезнание [Vseznanie] is not the most commonly used translation of *omniscience*. It has a touch of the pejorative about it, in the sense of *know-it-all-ism*. For the Soviet reader, in the context of despotism, this meaning will come to the fore to point disparagingly at Stalin, who was revered as the fount of all knowledge. This feature of Stalin's personality was immortalized in a song by Yuz Aleshkovskij, which began: "Comrade Stalin, you're a great academic (Товарищ Сталин! Вы – большой ученый [Tovarishch Stalin! Vy – bol'shoj uchenyj]). The image is evocative, and the formulation elegant. For the Soviet reader, the evil in the three goals of M&K's second-edition is ever so much more heinous than Tolkien's; ever so much more Soviet.

The first two of Volkovskij's three goals are exactly the same as G&G's: 'Knowledge, Power' [Знание, Власть]. His third goal, however, seems to be a throwback to M&K's first-edition, utopian goals. Volkovskij's Sauron tempts Gandalf with the possibility of achieving 'Common Harmony' [Всеобщий Лад] (V, F. 360).

Bobyr' and Yakhnin avoided this whole problem by omitting this dialog.

14 Conclusion

It is clear from the description above that the Russian book market offers its readers a much greater 'choice' than does the English-language book market. If a Russian reader does not have much time, and just wants the plot highlights, there are the Bobyr' and the Yakhnin re-tellings. If a Russian reader wants a Russian story instead of an English one, there are the M&K and the Volkovskij. If a Russian reader wants a new-age Tolkien, there is the G&G. If the Russian reader wants an annotated *LotR*, there is the K&K. If a Russian reader wants a text with all the big words simplified, there is the VAM. If the Russian reader wants to read Tolkien, however, they have to read him in the Original, and to help them get their English up to speed, there is the Gruzberg and the Nemirova. Choice is the hallmark of a market economy, and the Russians are obviously doing their best to become one.

About the author

Mark T. Hooker was a visiting scholar at Indiana University's Russian and East European Institute (REEI). He was the Key-note Speaker at the 'Concerning Hobbits and Other Matters: Tolkien Across the Disciplines', which was held at the University of St. Thomas in St. Paul, MN, in April, 2001. He was also one of the select international panel of speakers at the 4th Lustrum (20th Anniversary) of the Dutch Tolkien Society, Unquendor, in 2001. His articles on Tolkien have been published in English in *Beyond Bree*, *Vinyar Tengwar* and *Tolkien Studies*, in Dutch in *Lembas* (the journal of the Dutch Tolkien Society) and in Russian in *Palantir* (the journal of the St. Petersburg Tolkien Society). His monograph entitled *Tolkien Through Russian Eyes*, examining Russian Tolkienism in detail, has also been published by Walking Tree Publishers.

Bibliography of translations

BOBYR', Zinaida Anatol'evna (retold by), *Povest' o Kol'tse*, (her abridged and adapted retelling of *The Lord of the Rings* circulated in samizdat beginning in the mid-1960s).

Povest' o Kol'tse, Moscow: SP Interprint, 1990, 1991.

GRIGOR'EVA, Natalya, and Vladimir Grushetskij (trans.), *Vlastelin Kolets*, verse translated by I. Grinshpun. (In the 1980s, their translation of *The Two Towers* and *The Return of the King* circulated widely in samizdat, often in combination with the Gruzberg translation of *The Fellowship of the Ring*. The samizdat version (G&Gs) was considerably revised before going into print.)

Vlastelin Kolets, (one-volume edition), St. Petersburg: Severo-Zapad, 1991.

Bratstvo Kol'tsa, (volume 1 of the six-volume centenary edition of Tolkien's collected works), St. Petersburg: Severo-Zapad, 1992. (G&Gp)

Dve Kreposti, (volume 2 of the six-volume centenary edition of Tolkien's collected works), St. Petersburg: Severo-Zapad, 1992.

Vozvrashchenie Korolya, (volume 3 of the six-volume centenary edition of Tolkien's collected works), St. Petersburg: Severo-Zapad, 1992.

Vlastelin Kolets, (two-volume set), Moscow: TO Izdatel', 1993.

Vlastelin Kolets, (one-volume edition), St. Petersburg: Terra/Azbuka, 1996.

Bratstvo Kol'tsa, St. Petersburg: Azbuka, 2000.

Dve Kreposti, St. Petersburg: Azbuka, 2000.

Vozvrashchenie Korolya, St. Petersburg: Azbuka, 2000.

Vlastelin Kolets, (one-volume edition), St. Petersburg: Azbuka, 2000.

Vlastelin Kolets, (one-volume edition with the Rakhmanova translation of *The Hobbit*), St. Petersburg: Azbuka, 2000.

GRUZBERG, Aleksandr Abramovich (trans.), *Vlastelin kolets*, (The first Russian samizdat translation (1976). Verse translated by Yu. Batalina (née Gruzberg, his daughter). It was available on the Internet in three versions, A, B and C. It has since been pulled from the Internet at the request of the author. It was subsequently published in soft-copy on CD-ROM.)

Vlastelin Kolets, Moscow: IDDK, 2000.

KAMENKOVICH, Mariya (née Trofimchik) and Valerij Karrik (pseudonym: real name Kamenkovich) (trans.), *Sodruzhestvo Kol'tsa*, (fully annotated; prose translation and annotations by M. Kamenkovich and V. Karrik; verse translated by M. Kamenkovich and Sergej Stepanov. Afterword by M. Kamenkovich.) St. Petersburg: Terra/Azbuka, 1994.

Dve Bashni, St. Petersburg: Terra/Azbuka, 1994.

Vozvrashchenie Korolya, St. Petersburg: Terra/Azbuka, 1995.

Vlastelin Kolets: Kniga I: Sodruzhestvo Kol'tsa, St. Petersburg: Azbuka, 1999.

Vlastelin Kolets: Kniga II: Dve Bashni, St. Petersburg: Azbuka, 1999.

Vlastelin Kolets: Kniga III: Vozvrashchenie Korolya, St. Petersburg: Azbuka, 1999.

Vlastelin Kolets: Kniga I: Sodruzhestvo Kol'tsa, St. Petersburg: Amfora, 2000.

Vlastelin Kolets: Kniga II: Dve Bashni, St. Petersburg: Amfora, 2000.

Vlastelin Kolets: Kniga III: Vozvrashchenie Korolya, St. Petersburg: Amfora, 2000.

Vlastelin Kolets, (one-volume edition), St. Petersburg: Amfora, 2001.

Vlastelin Kolets: Kniga I: Sodruzhestvo Kol'tsa, (cover art is from the movie; issued as a set with *The Hobbit*) St. Petersburg: Amfora, 2002.

Vlastelin Kolets: Kniga II: Dve Bashni, St. Petersburg: Amfora, 2002.

Vlastelin Kolets: Kniga III: Vozvrashchenie Korolya, St. Petersburg: Amfora, 2002.

MATORINA, Valeriya Aleksandrovna (trans.), *Sodruzhestvo Kol'tsa*, Khabarovsk: Amur, 1991.

Dve Tverdyni, Khabarovsk: Amur, 1991.

Vozvrashchenie Korolya, Khabarovsk: Amur, 1991.

MURAV'EV, Vladimir, and Andrej Kistyakovskij (trans.), *Khraniteli*, (Abridged translation. Verse and all the names translated by A. Kistyakovskij.) Moscow: Detskaya Literatura, 1982. (M&K[1])

Khraniteli, (unabridged translation, prologue and translation of first book by Murav'ev) Moscow: Raduga, 1988, 1990, 1991. (M&K[2])

Dve Tverdyni, Moscow: Raduga, 1990.

Khraniteli, Ioshkar-ola: Marijskoe Knizhnoe Izdatel'stvo, 1992.

Dve Tverdyni, Novosibirsk: Knizhnoe Izdatel'stvo, 1992.

Vozvrashen'e Gosudarya, Moscow: Raduga, 1992.

Vozvrashen'e Gosudarya, Novosibirsk: Knizhnoe Izdatel'stvo, 1993.

Prilozheniya / Khraniteli, Baku: Olimp, 1993.

Dve Tverdyni / Vozvrashchenie Gosudarya, Baku: Olimp, 1993.

Khraniteli, (volume II of a four-volume set; volume I is the Rakhmanova translation of *The Hobbit*) Tula: Filin, 1994.

Dve Tverdyni, (volume III of a four-volume set) Tula: Filin, 1994.

Vozvrashchenie Gosudarya, (volume IV of a four-volume set) Tula: Filin, 1994.

Khraniteli, (illustrated by Leo Khao) Moscow: EKSMO-Press/Yauza, 1998.

Dve Tverdyni, Moscow: EKSMO-Press/Yauza, 1998.

Vozvrashchenie Gosudarya, Moscow: EKSMO-Press/Yauza, 1998.

Khraniteli, Moscow: Rosman-Press, 2000.

Dve Tverdyni, Moscow: Rosman-Izdat, 2000.

Vozvrashchenie Gosudarya, Moscow: Rosman-Izdat, 2000.

Vlastelin Kolets, (one-volume edition) Moscow: EKSMO-Press/Yauza, 2001.

NEMIROVA, Alina V. (trans.), *Khraniteli Kol'tsa*, Moscow: AST, Khar'kov: Folio, 2002.

Dve Tverdyni, Moscow: AST, Khar'kov: Folio, 2002.

Vozvrashchenie Korolya, Moscow: AST, Khar'kov: Folio, 2002.

VOLKOVSKIJ, Vitalij (trans.), *Druzhestvo Kol'tsa*, (verse translated by V. Vosedoj; part of a five-volume set, including the Estel' (Chertkova) translation of *The Silmarillion* and the Korolev translation of *The Hobbit*. Cover art by Greg and Tim Hildebrandt.) Moscow: AST, St. Petersburg: Terra Fantastika, 2000.

Dve Tverdyni, Moscow: AST, St. Petersburg: Terra Fantastika, 2000.

Vozvrashchenie Gosudarya, Moscow: AST, St. Petersburg: Terra Fantastika, 2000.

YAKHNIN, Leonid L. (retold by), *Khraniteli*, (illustrated by N. Kundukhov; cover art by T.N. Khromova) Moscow: Armada/Al'fa-kniga, 1999.

Dve Bashni, Moscow: Armada/Al'fa-kniga, 1999.

Vozvrashchenie Korolya, Moscow: Armada/Al'fa-kniga, 1999.

Khraniteli, Moscow: Armada/Al'fa-kniga, 2001.

Dve Bashni, Moscow: Armada/Al'fa-kniga, 2001.

Vozvrashchenie Korolya. Moscow: Armada/Al'fa-kniga, 2001.

Walking Tree Publishers

Walking Tree Publishers was founded in 1997 as a forum for publication of material (books, videos, CDs, etc.) related to Tolkien and Middle-earth studies. Manuscripts and project proposals can be submitted to the board of editors (please include an SAE):

Walking Tree Publishers
CH-3052 Zollikofen
Switzerland
e-mail: info@walking-tree.org
http://www.walking-tree.org

Cormarë Series

The *Cormarë Series* has been the first series of studies dedicated exclusively to the exploration of Tolkien's work. Its focus is on papers and studies from a wide range of scholarly approaches. The series comprises monographs, thematic collections of essays, conference volumes, and reprints of important yet no longer (easily) accessible papers by leading scholars in the field. Manuscripts and project proposals are evaluated by members of an independent board of advisors who support the series editors in their endeavour to provide the readers with qualitatively superior yet accessible studies on Tolkien and his work.

News from the Shire and Beyond. Studies on Tolkien
Peter Buchs and Thomas Honegger (eds.), Zurich and Berne 2004, Reprint, First edition 1997 (Cormarë Series 1), ISBN 978-3-9521424-5-5

Root and Branch. Approaches Towards Understanding Tolkien
Thomas Honegger (ed.), Zurich and Berne 2005, Reprint, First edition 1999 (Cormarë Series 2), ISBN 978-3-905703-01-6

Richard Sturch, *Four Christian Fantasists. A Study of the Fantastic Writings of George MacDonald, Charles Williams, C.S. Lewis and J.R.R. Tolkien*
Zurich and Berne 2007, Reprint, First edition 2001 (Cormarë Series 3), ISBN 978-3-905703-04-7

Tolkien in Translation
Thomas Honegger (ed.), Zurich and Jena 2011, Reprint, First edition 2003 (Cormarë Series 4), ISBN 978-3-905703-15-3

Mark T. Hooker, *Tolkien Through Russian Eyes*
Zurich and Berne 2003 (Cormarë Series 5), ISBN 978-3-9521424-7-9

Translating Tolkien: Text and Film
Thomas Honegger (ed.), Zurich and Jena 2011, Reprint, First edition 2004 (Cormarë Series 6), ISBN 978-3-905703-16-0

Christopher Garbowski, *Recovery and Transcendence for the Contemporary Mythmaker. The Spiritual Dimension in the Works of J.R.R. Tolkien*
Zurich and Berne 2004, Reprint, First Edition by Marie Curie Sklodowska, University Press, Lublin 2000, (Cormarë Series 7), ISBN 978-3-9521424-8-6

Reconsidering Tolkien
Thomas Honegger (ed.), Zurich and Berne 2005 (Cormarë Series 8),
ISBN 978-3-905703-00-9

Tolkien and Modernity 1
Frank Weinreich and Thomas Honegger (eds.), Zurich and Berne 2006 (Cormarë Series 9), ISBN 978-3-905703-02-3

Tolkien and Modernity 2
Thomas Honegger and Frank Weinreich (eds.), Zurich and Berne 2006 (Cormarë Series 10), ISBN 978-3-905703-03-0

Tom Shippey, *Roots and Branches. Selected Papers on Tolkien by Tom Shippey*
Zurich and Berne 2007 (Cormarë Series 11), ISBN 978-3-905703-05-4

Ross Smith, *Inside Language. Linguistic and Aesthetic Theory in Tolkien*
Zurich and Berne 2007 (Cormarë Series 12), ISBN 978-3-905703-06-1

How We Became Middle-earth. A Collection of Essays on The Lord of the Rings
Adam Lam and Nataliya Oryshchuk (eds.), Zurich and Berne 2007 (Cormarë Series 13), ISBN 978-3-905703-07-8

Myth and Magic. Art According to the Inklings
Eduardo Segura and Thomas Honegger (eds.), Zurich and Berne 2007 (Cormarë Series 14), ISBN 978-3-905703-08-5

The Silmarillion - Thirty Years On
Allan Turner (ed.), Zurich and Berne 2007 (Cormarë Series 15),
ISBN 978-3-905703-10-8

Martin Simonson, *The Lord of the Rings and the Western Narrative Tradition*
Zurich and Jena 2008 (Cormarë Series 16), ISBN 978-3-905703-09-2

Tolkien's Shorter Works. Proceedings of the 4th Seminar of the Deutsche Tolkien Gesellschaft & Walking Tree Publishers Decennial Conference
Margaret Hiley and Frank Weinreich (eds.), Zurich and Jena 2008 (Cormarë Series 17), ISBN 978-3-905703-11-5

Tolkien's The Lord of the Rings: Sources of Inspiration
Stratford Caldecott and Thomas Honegger (eds.), Zurich and Jena 2008 (Cormarë Series 18), ISBN 978-3-905703-12-2

J.S. Ryan, *Tolkien's View: Windows into his World*
Zurich and Jena 2009 (Cormarë Series 19), ISBN 978-3-905703-13-9

Music in Middle-earth
Heidi Steimel and Friedhelm Schneidewind (eds.), Zurich and Jena 2010 (Cormarë Series 20), ISBN 978-3-905703-14-6

Liam Campbell, *The Ecological Augury in the Works of JRR Tolkien*
Zurich and Jena 2011 (Cormarë Series 21), ISBN 978-3-905703-18-4

Margaret Hiley, *The Loss and the Silence. Aspects of Modernism in the Works of C.S. Lewis, J.R.R. Tolkien and Charles Williams*
Zurich and Jena 2011 (Cormarë Series 22), ISBN 978-3-905703-19-1

J.S. Ryan, *In the Nameless Wood* (working title)
Zurich and Jena, forthcoming

Rainer Nagel, *Hobbit Place-names. A Linguistic Excursion through the Shire*
Zurich and Jena, forthcoming

The Broken Scythe. Death and Immortality in the Works of J.R.R. Tolkien
Roberto Arduini and Claudio Antonio Testi (eds.), Zurich and Jena, forthcoming

Christopher MacLachlan, *Tolkien and Wagner: The Ring and Der Ring*
Zurich and Jena, forthcoming

Renée Vink, *Wagner and Tolkien*
Zurich and Jena, forthcoming

Constructions of Authorship in and around the Works of J.R.R. Tolkien
Judith Klinger (ed.), Zurich and Jena, forthcoming

Tolkien's Poetry
Julian Morton Eilmann and Allan Turner (eds.), Zurich and Jena, forthcoming

Beowulf and the Dragon

The original Old English text of the 'Dragon Episode' of *Beowulf* is set in an authentic font and printed and bound in hardback creating a high quality art book. The text is illustrated by Anke Eissmann and accompanied by John Porter's translation. The introduction is by Tom Shippey. Limited first edition of 500 copies. 84 pages. Selected pages can be previewed on: www.walking-tree.org/beowulf
Beowulf and the Dragon
Zurich and Jena 2009, ISBN 978-3-905703-17-7

Tales of Yore Series

The *Tales of Yore Series* grew out of the desire to share Kay Woollard's whimsical stories and drawings with a wider audience. The series aims at providing a platform for qualitatively superior fiction with a clear link to Tolkien's world.

Kay Woollard, *The Terror of Tatty Walk. A Frightener*
CD and Booklet, Zurich and Berne 2000, ISBN 978-3-9521424-2-4

Kay Woollard, *Wilmot's Very Strange Stone or What came of building "snobbits"*
CD and booklet, Zurich and Berne 2001, ISBN 978-3-9521424-4-8

www.ingramcontent.com/pod-product-compliance
Lightning Source LLC
Chambersburg PA
CBHW050822160426
43192CB00010B/1867